# TWO PLAYS BY ALEISTER CROWLEY

*Tannhäuser & Household Gods*

# Other Titles from AZ Classics

*All titles priced at $15.99 each*
*Shipping & handling:* **$4.99 for the first book, $0.99 for each additional book**

## Titles Available:

- The Beetle – Richard Marsh
- **Convict B14 – R.K. Weekes**
- *The House Behind the Cedars* – Charles W. Chesnutt
- *Jill* – E.A. Dillwyn
- Lolla: Or The Sin of Greediness – Lucy Ellen Guernsey
- *The Man* – Bram Stoker
- The Mummy: A Tale of the 22$^{nd}$ Century – Jane Webb Loudon

To order, send a list of the titles
and a check or money order to:

**AZ Entertainment Group LLC**
**PO BOX 854**
**Wagoner, OK 74477**

Books also available online at
az-entertainmentllc.com/order

# TWO PLAYS BY ALEISTER CROWLEY

*Tannhäuser & Household Gods*

Classics

Wagoner Oklahoma

Published by AZ Classics
An imprint of AZ Entertainment Group LLC

ISBN: 978-1-947035-62-1

Edited by Richard Leighland
Cover Design by AZ Classics

For inquiries, including bulk orders of 100 or more, please contact:
AZ Entertainment Group LLC
PO BOX 854
Wagoner, OK 74477-0854
Email: info@az-entertainmentllc.com
Website: www.az-entertainmentllc.com

Printed in the United States of America

# Table of Contents

# INTRODUCTION

Aleister Crowley is remembered in popular culture as "the wickedest man in the world," a magician, and self-styled prophet of the new Aeon. Yet he was also a serious writer and an artist whose literary output ranges from lyric poetry to philosophical treatises. His notoriety has often overshadowed his other pursuits. The plays gathered here reveal a different side of Crowley: the dramatist. These plays prove he could shock and mesmerize without a single spell, but perhaps they were the spell.

*Tannhäuser* and *Household Gods* could hardly be more different in form and tone. *Tannhäuser* draws on medieval legend and Wagnerian associations, and unfolds in a lofty, mystical register. It is rich in symbolism, erotic undercurrents, and the search for transcendence. *Household Gods*, by contrast, is a modern, satirical play rooted in the banality of domestic life. What begins as a comedy of manners twists into a sharp critique of materialism and a meditation on the divine hidden in the everyday.

Despite their differences, the two works share a common concern: transformation. Crowley's characters wrestle with the conflict between worldly desire and spiritual vision, between the comfort of convention and the risk of awakening. These are not merely occult curiosities but ambitious theatrical works that reflect his broader artistic project: to provoke and illuminate.

Taken together, these plays demonstrate Crowley was more than an occultist and more than a scandalous personality. He was an artist whose dramatic voice, by turns lyrical and biting, deserves to be read on its own terms.

Richard Leighland, Editor

# THE PLAYS

# TANNHÄUSER

## A STORY OF ALL TIME

# TANNHÄUSER

### XVI

One is incisive, corrosive;
Two retorts, nettled, curt, crepitant;
Three makes rejoinder, expansive, explosive;
Four overbears them all, strident and strepitant:
Five ... O Danaides, O Sieve!

### XVII

Now, they ply axes and crowbars;
Now, they prick pins at a tissue
Fine as a skein of the casuist Escobar's
Worked on the bone of a lie. To what issue?
Where is our gain at the Two-bars?

### XVIII

*Est fuga, volvitur rota.*
On we drift: where looms the dim port?
One, Two, Three, Four, Five, contribute their quota;
Something is gained, if one caught but the import—
Show it us, Hughes of Saxe-Gotha!

R. BROWNING, *Master Hughes of Saxe-Gotha*

# DEDICATION

I SHALL not tell thee that I love thee!
Nay! by the Star in Heaven burning,
Its ray to me at midnight turning
To tell me that it beams above thee—
Nay! though thou wert, as I am, yearning,
I should not tell thee that I love thee!
I know what secret thought once blossomed
Into a blush that seemed a kiss,
Some swift suppressed extreme of bliss
In thy most fearful sigh embosomed.
What oracle should prate of this?
I know the secret thought that blossomed!
Extol the truth of love's disdain!
Love, daring by no glance to gladden
      A heart that waits but that to madden
In purple pleasure plucked of pain.
Nay! let our tears, that fail to sadden,
Extol the truth of love's disdain!

\*\*\*

Let deeper silence shield the deeper rapture!
Hardly our eyes reveal the inward bliss,
Sealed by no speech and shadowed by no kiss.
Love is no wizard to elude recapture
In the strong prison of his silences!

15

Let deeper silence shield the deeper rapture!
Twin souls are we, to one Star bound in Heaven!
Twin souls on earth by earthly bars divided!
But, did thy spirit glide as mine has glided
Straight to That Star—no rose-leaves ask to leaven
The manna that the Moon of Love provided!
Twin souls are we, to one Star bound in Heaven!
Not to thy presence in the veil and vision
Of solemn lies that men miscall the world;
Not to thy mind the lightnings truthward hurled
I turn. I laugh dead distance to derision!—
Spirit to spirit: there our loves are curled,
Not to thy presence in the veil and vision!
Beyond the gold and glamour of Life's lotus,
The flower that falls from this our stronger sight,
We dwell, eternal shapes of shadowy light.
Only the love on earth that shook and smote us
Begets new stars—truth's flowers fallen through night
Beyond the gold and glamour of Life's lotus!
Eternal bliss of Love in birthless bowers!
Light, the gemmed robes of Love! Life, lifted breath,
Ageless existence deifying death!
Love, the sole flower beyond these lesser flowers!—
In thee at last the live fruit quickeneth?
Eternal bliss of Love in birthless bowers!

\*\*\*

There, secret! Know it! Now forget!
Betray not Wisdom unto Folly!
Less sweet is Joy than Melancholy!—
Why should our eyes for this be wet?

Enough: be silent and be holy!
There, secret! Know it! Now forget!
Now I have told thee that I love thee!
To me our Star in Heaven burning
Tells me thy heart as mine is yearning;
Tells me Love's fragrance stolen above thee
Thy soul to mine at last is turning
Now I have told thee that I love thee!

# PREFACE

As, after long observation and careful study, the biologist sees that what at first seemed isolated and arbitrary acts are really part of a series of regular changes, and presently has the life-history of the being that he is examining clear from Alpha to Omega in his mind; as, during a battle, the relative importance of its various incidents is lost, the more so owing to the excitement and activity of the combatant, and to the fact that he is himself involved in the vicissitudes which he may have set himself to observe; while even for the commander, though the smoke-pall may lift now and again to show some brilliant charge or desperate hand-to-hand struggle, he may fail to grasp its significance in his dispositions; or indeed find it to be quite unexpected and foreign to his calculations; yet a few years or months later the same battle may be lucidly, tersely, and connectedly described, so that a child is able to follow its varying fortunes with delight and comprehension: just so has my own observation of a life-history more subtle, a battle more terrible, been at last co-ordinated: I can view the long struggle from a standpoint altogether complete, calm, and philosophical; and the result of this review is the present story of Tannhäuser, just as the isolated and often apparently contradictory incidents of the fight were recorded in that jungle of chaotic emotions which I printed under the title of "The Soul of Osiris," calling it a history so that my readers might discover for themselves (if they chose to take the trouble) the real continuity in the apparent disjointedness.

The history of any man who seriously and desperately dares to force a passage into the penetralia of nature; not with the calm philosophy of the scientist, but with the burning conviction that his immortal destiny is at stake; must be a strange one: to me at least strangely attractive. The constant illusions; the many disappointments; the bitter earnestness of the man amid the grim humour, or more often sheer cacchination of his surroundings; all the bestial mockery of the baffling fiends; the still more hideous mockery in which the Powers of Good themselves seem to indulge; doubt of the reality of that which he seeks; doubt even of the seeker; the irony of the whole strife: are fascinating to me as they are, I make no doubt, to the majority of mankind.

This is the subtler form of that mental bewilderment which the Greek Tragedians were so fond of depicting; as subtle in effect, yet grosser in its determining factors. For we are thus changed from the times of Sophocles and Euripides; that the fixed ideas of morality and religion which they employed as the motives of pathos or of horror are now shattered. Ibsen, otherwise in spirit and style purely Greek, and dealing as the Greeks did with the emotions of the soul, has realised the changed and infinitely more complex conditions of life; our self-appointed spiritual guides notwithstanding, or, rather, withstanding in vain. Consequently it is impossible any more to divine whether virtue or vice (as understood of old) will cause the irreparable catastrophe which is the one element of drama which we may still (in the work of a modern dramatist) await with any degree of confidence.

I trust that I may be forgiven for adopting the idea that Tannhäuser was one of those mysterious Germans whose reputed existence so perturbed the Middle Ages; in short, a Rosicrucian. Some people may be surprised that a Member of that illustrious but unhappy fraternity should take cognizance of what my friend Bhikku Ananda Mîtriya calls "hognosed Egyptian deities," still more that he should show reverence to symbols like the B. V. M. and the Holy Grail. But the most learned and profound students of the Mysteries of the Rosy Cross assure me that it was the special excellence of these mystics that they declined to be bound down by any particular system in their sublime search for the Eternal and the

Real.

Under these circumstances I have not scrupled to subvert anything that appeared to me to need subverting in the interests, always identical, of beauty and of truth. Anachronism may be found piled upon anachronism, and symbolism mixed with symbolism.

In one direction I have restrained myself. Nowhere does Tannhäuser refer to the Vedas and Shastras or to the Dhamma of that blameless hypochondriac, Gotama Buddha. I take all the blame for so important an omission, not without a shrewd suspicion that the commination will take the form of "For this relief much thanks!"

The particular object that I have in view in speaking both in Hebrew and Egypto-Christian symbology is that by this means I may familiarise my readers with the one thing of any importance that life, travel, and study have taught me, to wit: the Origin of Religions.

I take it that there have always, or nearly always, been on the earth those whom Councillor von Eckartshäusen, the Svámi Vivekánanda and their like, call "great spiritual giants" (can there be any etymological link between "yogi" and "ogre"?) and that such persons, themselves perceiving Truth, have tried to "diminish the message to the dog" for the benefit of less exalted minds, and hidden that Truth (which, unveiled, would but blind men with its glory) in a mass of symbology often perverted or grotesque, yet to the proper man transparent; a "bait of falsehood to catch the carp of truth." Now, regarded in this light, all religions, quá religions, are equally contemptible. The Hindu Gnanis say "That which can be thought is not true." As machineries for the exercise of spiritual and intellectual powers innate or developed, certain sets of symbols may be more or less convenient to a special trend of mind, reason, or imagination; no more: I deny to any one religion the possession of any essential truth which is not also formulated (though in a different language) in every other. To this rule Buddhism appears a solitary exception. Whether it is truly so I have hardly yet decided: the answer depends upon certain recondite mathematical considerations, to discuss which would be foreign to the scope of my present purpose, but which I hope to advance in a subsequent volume.

If you do not accept my conclusion that all religions are the expression of truth under different aspects, facets of the same intolerable gem, you are forced back on the conclusions of those unpleasing persons the Phallicists. But should you travel to the East, and tell a Lingam-worshipping Sivite that his is a phallic worship he will not be pleased with you. Compare on this point Arnold, "India Revisited," 1886, p. 112.

So much for the symbology of this, I fear, much-mangled drama. Drama indeed is an altogether misleading term; monodrama is perhaps better. It is really a series of introspective studies; not necessarily a series in time, but in psychology, and that rather the morbid psychology of the Adept than the gross mentality of the ordinary man.

It may help some of my readers if I say that my Tannhäuser is nearly identical in scheme with the "Pilgrim's Progress." Literary and spiritual experts will however readily detect minor differences in the treatment. It will be sufficient if I state that "the Unknown," whether minstrel, pilgrim, or Egyptian sage, represents Tannhäuser in his true Self,—the "Only Being in an Abyss of Light!" The Tannhäuser who talks is the "Only Being in an Abyss of Darkness," the natural man ignorant of his identity with the Supreme Being. The various other characters are all little parts of Tannhäuser's own consciousness and not real persons at all: whether good or bad, all alike hinder and help (and there is not one whose function is not thus double) the realisation of his true unity with all life. This circumstance serves to explain, though perhaps not to excuse, the lack of dramatic action in the story. Love being throughout the symbol of his method, as Beauty of its object, it is through Love, refined into Pity, that he at last attains the Supreme Knowledge, or at least sufficient of it to put the last straw on the back of his corporeal camel, and bring the story to a fitting end.

To pass to more mundane affairs. I may mention for the benefit of those who may not be read in certain classes of literature, and so think me original when I am hardly even paraphrasing, that Tannhäuser's songs in Act IV. are partly adapted from the so-called "Oracles of Zoroaster," partly from the mysterious utterances of the great angel Avé, perhaps equally spurious. Of course Bertram's song is merely a rather free adaptation of the two principal fragments of Sappho, which so many people have failed to translate that one can feel no shame in making yet another attempt. There may be one or two conscious plagiarisms besides, for which I do not apologise. For any unconscious ones which may have crept in owing to my prolonged absence from civilized parts, and the consequent lack of opportunity for reference and comparison, I emphatically do.

One word to the reviewers. It must not be taken as ungracious if I so speak. From nearly all I have received the utmost justice, kindness, and consideration: two or three only seem to take delight in deliberately perverting the sense of my remarks: and to them, for their own sake, I now address these words of elementary instruction. You are perfectly welcome to do with my work in its entirety what Laertes did with his allegiance and his vows: but do not pick out and gloat over a few isolated passages from the Venusberg scenes and call me a sensualist, nor from the Fourth Act and groan "Mysticism!"; do not quote "Two is by shape the Coptic Aspirate" as a sample of my utmost in lyrics; do not take the song of Wolfram as my best work in either sentiment or melody. As a *quid pro quo* I give you all full permission to conclude your review of this book by quoting from Act III. "Forget this nightmare!"

I must express my great sense of gratitude to Oscar Eckenstein, Gerald Kelly, and Allan MacGregor, who have severally helped me in the work of revision, which has extended over more than a year of time and nearly twenty thousand miles of space. Some few of the very best lines were partially or wholly suggested by themselves, and I have not scrupled to incorporate these: if the book be but a Book, the actual authorship seems to me immaterial.

I have written this preface in lighter vein, but I hope that no one will be led to suppose that my purpose is anything but deadly serious. This poem has been written in the blood of slain faith and hope; each foolish utterance of Tannhäuser stings me with shame and memory of old agony; each Ignis Fatuus that he so readily pursues, reminds me of my own delusions. But, these follies and delusions being the common property of mankind, I have thought them of sufficient interest, dramatic and philosophical, to form the basis of a poem. Let no man dare to reproach me with posing as the hero of my tale. I fall back on the last utterance of Tannhäuser himself "I say, then, 'I': and yet it is not 'I' Distinct, but 'I' incorporate in All." Above all, pray understand that I do not pose as a teacher. I am but an asker of questions, such as may be found confronting those who have indeed freed their minds from the conventional commonplaces of the platitudinous, but have not yet dared to uproot the mass of their convictions, and to examine the whole question of religion from its most fundamental source in the consciousness of mankind. Such persons may find the reasoning of Tannhäuser useful, if only to brace them to a more courageous attempt to understand the "Great Arcanum," and to attain at last, no matter at what cost, to "true Wisdom and perfect Happiness." So may all happen!

KANDY, CEYLON, *Sept.* 1901.

# TANNHÄUSER

## PERSONS CONCERNED

### THE WORLD OF GODS

Isis
Hathoör

### THE WORLD OF MEN

Tannhäuser
Elizabeth
An Unknown Minstrel
The Landgrave
Wolfram

### (at the Court of the Landgrave)

Bertram
Heinrich
A Shepherd-Boy
Pilgrims, Foresters, Courtiers, etc.

### THE WORLD OF DEMONS

The Evil and Averse Hathoör, called Venus

# ACT I.

"Therefore we are carefully to proceed in Magic, lest that Syrens and other monsters deceive us, which likewise do desire the society of the human soul."

Arbatel of Magic.    Aphorism 35.

A lonely and desolate plain. Tannhäuser riding towards a great mountain.

### Tannhäuser.

SIX days. Creation took no longer! Yet
I wander eastward, and no light is found.
The stars their motion shirk, or else forget.
The sun—the moon? Imprisoned underground!
Where gnomes disport, and devils do abound.

Six days. I journey to the black unknown,
Always in hope the Infinite may rise
Some unexpected instant, as 'twere grown
A magic palace to enchanted eyes;
A wizard guerdon for a minstrel wise.

Perhaps I am a fool to think that here,
Merely by rending Nature's hollow veil,
I may attain the Solitary Sphere,
　　Achieve the Path; or, haply, if I fail,
Gain the Elixir, or behold the Grail.

I seek the mystery of Life and Time,
The Key of all that is not and that is,
And that which—climb, imagination! climb!—
Transcends them both—the mystical abyss
Where Mind and Being marry, and are Bliss.

So have I journeyed—like a fool! Ah, well!
Let pass self-scorn, as love of self is past!
But—am I further forward? Who can tell?
God is the Complex as the Protoplast:
He is the First (not "was"), and is the Last

(Not "will be"). Then why travel? To what end?
What is the symbol I am set to find?
What is that burning heart of blood to spend
Caught in a sunset with the night behind,
The Grail of God? I would that I were blind!

I would that I were desolate and dumb,
Naked and poor! That He might manifest
A crimson glory subtly caught and come,
An opal crucible of Alkahest!
And yet—what gain of vital gold expressed?

This were my guerdon: to fade utterly
Into the rose-heart of that sanguine vase,
And lose my purpose in its silent sea,

And lose my life, and find my life, and pass
Up to the sea that is as molten glass.

I mind me of that old Egyptian,
Met where Aurora streamed her rainbow hair,
Who called me from the quest. An holy man!
A crown of light scintillant in the air
Shone over him: he bade me not despair.

"The Blood of the Osiris" was his word:
(Meaning the Christ?) "The life, the tears, the tomb!
The Love of Isis is its name!" (I heard
This for the love of Mary.) In her womb
Brews the Elixir, and the roses bloom.

For the Three Maries (so he said) were One:
Three aspects of the mystic spouse of God,
Isis! This pagan! "Look towards the Sun"
(Quoth he) "And seek a winepress to be trod;
With Beauty girdled, garlanded, and shod."

"Thus," riddled he, "thy heart shall know its Peace!"
Let be! I ride upon the sand instead,
Look to the Cross, whereon I take mine ease!
Let be! Just so the Roman soldier said.
Esaias? He is dead—as I am dead!

What was his symbol and his riddle's key?
Go, seek the stars and count them and explore!
Go, sift the sands beyond a starless sea!
So, find an answer where the dismal shore
Of time beats back eternity! No more!

Let me ride on more hastily than this,
That so my body may be tired of me,
And fling me to the old forgetful kiss,
Sleep's, when my mind goes, riderless and free,
Into some corner of eternity.

Alas! that mind returns from its abode
With newer problems, fiercer thoughts! But stay!
Suppose it came not? It must be with God!—
Then this dull house of gold and iron and clayIs
happy also—'tis an easy way!

So easy, I am fearful of mishap.
Some fatal argument the God must find
That linked us first. The dice are in His lap—
Let Him decide in His imperial mind!
My choice; to see entirely—and be blind!

Yet I bethink me of that holy man,
(Pagan albeit) my stirrup's wisdom-share:
"Learn this from Thothmes the Egyptian.
Use only in thine uttermost despair!"
He whispered me a Word. "Beware! Beware!"

"Two voices are there in the sullen sea;
Two functions hath the inevitable fire;
Earthquake hath earth, and yet fertility:
See to thy purpose, and thy set desire!
Else, dire the fate—the ultimation dire!"

Vague threats and foolish words! Quite meaningless
The empty sounds he muttered in mine ear.
Why should their silly mystery impress

My thoughtful forehead with the lines of fear?
(This riding saps my courage as my cheer.)

Still, I must see his symbol of the Sun,
The Winepress, and the Beauty! Puerile
And pagan to that old mysterious one,
The awful Light and the anointed Vial,
The Dawning of the Blood, even as a smile:—

Even as a smile on Beauty's burning cheek—
Ha! In a circle? As this journey is?
How vain is man's imagining and weak!
Begod my lady, and my lady's kiss?
Back swing we to the pitiful abyss.

Liken God's being to the life of man.
So reason staggers. Angels, answer me!
Ye who have watched the far unfolding plan—
How is time shorter than eternity?
Prove it and weigh! By mind it cannot be.

All our divisions spring in our own brain.
See! As upsprings on the horizon there
A clefted hill contemptuous of the plain.
(Why, which is higher?) I am in despair.
Let me essay the Pharaoh and his prayer!
    [*Tannhäuser speaks the Word of Double Power.*]

Oh God, Thy blinding beauty, and the light
Shed from Thy shoulders, and the golden night
Of mingling fire and stars and roses swart
In the long flame of hair that leaps athwart,
Live in each tingling gossamer! Dread eyes!

Each flings its arrow of sharp sacrifice,
Eating me up with poison! I am hurled
Far through the vaporous confines of the world
With agony of sundering sense, beholding
Thy mighty flower, blood-coloured death, unfold-
ing!
Lithe limbs and supple shoulders and lips curled,
Curled out to draw me to their monstrous world!
Warm breasts that glow with light ephemeral
And move with passionate music to enthrall,
To charm, to enchant, to seal the entrancing breath.
I fall! Stop! Spare me!—Slay me!

[*Tannhäuser enters into an ecstasy.*]

This is death.

[*The evil and averse Hathoör, or Venus, who hath arisen in the place of the Great Goddess, lifteth up her voice and chanteth*:

—

**Venus.**


Isis am I, and from my life are fed
All showers and suns, all moons that wax and wane,
All stars and streams, the living and the dead,
The mystery of pleasure and of pain.
I am the mother! I the speaking sea!
I am the earth and its fertility!
Life, death, love, hatred, light, darkness, return to
me—
To me!

Hathoör am I, and to my beauty drawn
All glories of the Universe bow down,
The blossom and the mountain and the dawn,

Fruit's blush, and woman, our creation's crown.
I am the priest, the sacrifice, the shrine,
I am the love and life of the divine!
Life, death, love, hatred, light, darkness are surely
mine—
Are mine!

Venus am I, the love and light of earth,
The wealth of kisses, the delight of tears,
The barren pleasure never come to birth,
The endless, infinite desire of years.
I am the shrine at which thy long desire
Devoured thee with intolerable fire.
I was song, music, passion, death, upon thy lyre—
Thy lyre!

I am the Grail and I the Glory now:
I am the flame and fuel of thy breast;
I am the star of God upon thy brow;
I am thy queen, enraptured and possessed.
Hide thee, sweet river; welcome to the sea,
Ocean of love that shall encompass thee!
Life, death, love, hatred, light, darkness, return
to me—
To me!

[*Tannhäuser perceives that he is in the palace
of a Great Queen.*]

Rise, rise, my knight! My king! My love, arise!
See the grave avenues of Paradise,
The dewy larches bending at my breath,
Portentous cedars prophesying death!

See the long vistas and the dancing sea,
The measured motion of fecundity!
Bright winds set swaying the soft-sounding flowers
(Here flowers have music) in my woven bowers,
Where sweet birds blossom, and in chorus quire
The rapt beginnings of immense desire.
Here is the light and rapture of the will:
We touch the stars—and they are tiny still!
O mighty thews! O godlike face and hair!
Rise up and take me; ay, and keep me there,
One tingle at thy touch from head to feet;
Lips that cling close, and never seem to meet,
Melting as sunlight melts in wine! Arise!
Shame! Has thy learning left thee overwise?
Thy lips sing fondly—to another tune.
Nay! 'twas my breathing beauty made thee swoon,
Dread forkéd fire across the cloven sky;
Stripped off thy body of mortality—
Nay, but on steeper slopes my love shall strive!
Our bodies perish and our hearts revive
Vainly, unless the shaking sense beware
The crested snakes shot trembling through our hair,
Their wisdom! But our souls leap, flash, unite,
One crownéd column of avenging light,
Fixed and yet floating, infinite, immense,
Caught in the meshes of the cruel sense,
Two kissing breaths of agony and pleasure,
Mixed, crowned, divided, beyond age or measure,
Time, thought, or being! Now thine eyes awake,
Droop at my kisses; the long lashes slake
Their sleek and silky thirst in tears of light!
Thine eyes! They burn me, even me! They smite
Me who am scatheless, and a flame of fire.

See, in our sorrow and intense desire
All worlds are caught and sealed! The stars are taken
In love's weak web, and gathered up, and shaken!
Our word is mighty on the magic moon!
The sun resurges to our triple tune!
(See, it is done!) O chosen of the Christ!
My knight, and king, and lover, wast thou priced,
A portion in the all-pervading bliss,
Thou, whom I value at my ageless kiss?
Chosen of Me! Thou heart of hearts, thou mine,
Man! Stamping into dust the Soul Divine
By might of that mere Manhood! Sense and thought
Reel for the glory of thee kissed and caught
In the eternal circle of my arms!
Woven in vain are the mysterious charms
Endymion taught Diana! For one gaze;
One word of my unutterable praise;
And I was utterly and ever lost,
Lost in the whirlwind of thy love, and tossed
A wreck on its irremeable sea!
Life! Life! This kiss! Draw in thy breath! To me!
      To me!                 *[Tannhäuser is lost.]*

# ACT II.

"But a moment's thought is passion's passing bell."
—KEATS, *Lamia*.

## *In Venusberg.*

### Venus.

SWEET, sweet are May and June, dear,
The loves of lambent spring,
Our lamp the drooping moon, dear,
Our roof, the stars that sing;
The bed, of moss and roses;
The night, as long as death!
Still, breath!
Life wakens and reposes,
Love ever quickeneth!

Sweet, sweet, when Lion and Maiden,
The motley months of gold,
Swoop down with sunlight laden,
And eyes are bright and bold.
Life-swelling breasts uncover

Their warm involving deep—
Love, sleep!—
And lover lies with lover
On air's substantial steep.

### Tannhäuser.

Ah! sweeter was September—
The amber rain of leaves,
The harvest to remember,
The load of sunny sheaves.
In gardens deeply scented,
In orchards heavily hung,
Love flung
Away the days demented
With lips that curled and clung.

Ah! Sweeter still October,
When russet leaves go grey,
And sombre loves and sober
Make twilight of the day.
Dark dreams and shadows tenser
Throb through the vital scroll,
Man's soul,
Lift, shake the subtle censer
That hides the cruel coal!

Still sweeter when the Bowman
His silky shaft of frost
Lets loose on earth, that no man
May linger nor be lost.
The barren woods, deserted,
Lose echo of our sighs—

Love—dies?—
Love lives—in granite skirted,
And under oaken skies.

But best is grim December,
The Goatish God his power;
The Satyr blows the ember,
And pain is passion's flower;
When blood drips over kisses,
And madness sobs through wine:—
Ah, mine!—
The snake starts up and hisses
And strikes and—I am thine!

**Venus.**

Those are thy true joys? Cruelty for love?

**Tannhäuser.**

And death in kissing. How I have despised,
Riding through meadows of the rushing Rhine,
To watch the gentle foresters of spring
Crush dainty violets in their dalliance,
Laughing in chorus with the birds; and then
(Coming at harvest time upon my tracks)
See these same lovers in the golden sheaves
Under the sun. The same, the fuller fruit,
Say you? But somehow, nearer to the end,
Lost the old sense of mystery, and lost
That curious reverence in sacrilege
With Wonder—the child's faculty! Less joy,
Less laughter, yes! that symptom I approve;

Yet is that subtle fading-out of smiles
Rather the coming of a dull despair,
And not at all that keen despair, that sharp
Maddening pain that should torment a man
With deadliest delight, the self-same hour
That he unveils the Isis of desire.
These little lovers strip their maidens bare,
And find them—naked! Poor and pitiful!
Look at our love instead! I raised Thy veil,
Nay, tore Thy vesture from Thee, and behold!
Then only did I see what mystery,
What ninefold forest, shade impassible,
Surrounds Thy heart, as with a core of light
Shut in the mystery of a dead world.
Thou formless sense of gloom and terror! Thou
Upas, new tree of life—by sinister
Cherubim with averted faces kept!
Nay! This one secret I suspect, and gloat
Over the solemn purport of the dream
With subtle shuddering of joy,—and that
Keener delight, a sense of deadly fear!
This secret: Thou art darkness in Thyself,
And evil wrapped in light, and ugliness
Vested in beauty! Therefore is my love
No petty passion like these country-folk's:
No fertile glory (as the Love of God):
But vast and barren as the winter sea,
Holding I know not what enormous soul
In its salt bitter bosom, underneath
The iron waters and the serpent foam;
Below, where sight and sound are set no more,
But only the intolerable weight
Of its own gloomy selfhood. This am I:

This passion, lion-mouthed and adder-eyed.
A mass compressed, a glowing central core,
Like molten metal in the crucible!
Death's secret is some sweetness ultimate,
Sweeter than poison. Ah! My very words,
Chance phrases, ravel out the tale for me—
Sweetness and death—poison and love. Consider
How this same striving to the Infinite,
Which I intend by "love," is likest to
That journey's wonder to the womb of death:
Because no soul of man has ever crossed
Again that River—the old fable's wrong;
Æneas came never to the ghostly side!
Was not the boat weighed with his body still?
Felt he the keen emotions of the dead?
Could he, the mortal and the warrior,
Converse with Them, and understand? Believe!
No soul has crossed in utter sympathy
And yet returned; because of this decree:
No man can look upon the face of God!
Yet Moses looked upon His hinder parts,
And I—yes, goddess! in this passionate
Life in our secret mountain, well I know
Thy beauty, and Thy love, (although they be
Infinite, far beyond the mortal mind,
Body, or soul to touch, to comprehend,
And dwell in) that the utter intimate
Knowledge of Thee, if once I ravelled out
Thy secret, laid Thee naked to the bone—
Nay, to the marrow! were to come, aware,
Face to face full with deity itself.
And this I strive at! Therefore is my love
Wholly in tune with that concealed desire

Bred in each mortal, though he never know,
(Few do know) to transcend the bound of things,
And find in Death the purpose of this life.

### Venus.

Yes, there you tear one veil away from me!
Yet, am not I the willing one? Indeed
I feel the wonder of that same desire
From mine own side of the Impassible.
See then how equal God and man are made!
For I have clothed me in the veil of flesh,
And strive toward thy finite consciousness
As thou art reaching to my infinite,
Nurturing my Godhead at the breast of Sin
With milk of fleshly stings—even to pain:—

### Tannhäuser.

I see, I see the Christian mystery!
That was the purpose of High God Himself,
Clothed in the Christ! Ah! Triumphed He at last?
Nay, not in death! The slave—He rose again!
Alas! Alas!

### Venus.

Alas indeed, my knight!
We love not! Being both enamoured of
Just the one thing that is impossible.
But in this carnal strife the Intimate
Achieves for one snatched swiftness. Kiss me, love!

### Tannhäuser.

Ah, but the waking! As I sink to sleep
Pillowed in nuptial arms—so fresh and cool—
(Yet in their veins I know the fire that runs
Racing and maddening from the crown of flame,
The monolithic core of mystical
Red fury that is called a woman's heart)
Sinking, I say, from the supreme embrace,
The Good-night kisses; sinking into sleep—
What dreams betoken the dread solitude?

### Venus.

What dreams? Ah, dreamest not of me, my knight?
Of vast caresses that include all worlds?
Of transmutation into molten steel
Fusing with my intolerable gold
In the red crucible of alchemy,
That is—of clay?

### Tannhäuser.

I dream of no such thing.
But of Thy likeness have I often seen
The vast presentment—formless, palpable,
Breathing. Not breathing as we use the word,
When life and spirit mingle in one breath,
Slay passion in one kiss—breathing, I say,
Differently from Thee!

43

**Venus.**

Explain, explain!

**Tannhäuser.**

As if were kindled into gold and fire
The East!

**Venus.**

The East!

**Tannhäuser.**

As if a flowerless moss
Suddenly broke in passionate primroses!

**Venus.**

Violets, violets!

**Tannhäuser.**

Or as if a man
Lay in the fairest garden of the world,
In the beginning: and grew suddenly
A living soul at that caressing wind!

**Venus.**

A living soul!

**Tannhäuser.**

So is Thy shade to me
When sleep takes shape.

**Venus.**

She is mine enemy
Hate her, O hate her, she will slay thy soul!

**Tannhäuser.**

And is my soul not slain within me now?
Yet, I do hate her—in these waking hours.
But in my sleep she grows upon the sense,
A solitary lotus that pales forth
In the wide seas of space and separateness.
That radiance!—Amber-scented voice of light,
Calling my name, ever, ever calling—

**Venus.**

Answer that call—and thou art lost indeed!
Wake thou thy spirit in this hateful sleep,
Keeping the vision, rise, and spit on her!

**Tannhäuser.**

Spit on Thy likeness? I who love Thee so?

**Venus.**

Yes, yes: obey me! She will leave thee then.

She hath assumed mine image! [*Thunder.*]

### Tannhäuser.

What is that?

### Venus.

Mere thunder on the mountain top. Do this,
And I will come in sleep, in sleep renew
The carnal joys of day.

### Tannhäuser.

Hast Thou forgot?
It is the fleshly I would flee!

### Venus.

Forget?
But I strive fleshwards. Let our sleep renew
The endless struggle—and perhaps, for thee,
For thee!—the veil may lift another fold.

### Tannhäuser.

Why dost Thou hate this vision?

### Venus.

She would take

Thee from these arms!

### Tannhäuser.

But she is beautiful
With Thine own beauty: yet as if the God
Cancelled its mortal comeliness, and came
More intimate than matter, closing in
Keen on my spirit; as if all I sought
In Thine own symbol, Beauty, were concealed
Under her brows—how wider than the air!
How deeper than the sea! How radiant
Beyond the fire!

### Venus.

O shun her devilish lures!
That Beauty is the sole detested fear
That can annul our conquests, and arouse
Our rapt dream-kisses.

### Tannhäuser.

That is my intent.
It is the spiritual life of things
I seek—Thou knowest!

### Venus.

Oh, I did not mean!
Remember my dilemma! Hear me speak
The story of her. She is a wicked witch
That seeketh to delude thy sleepy sense

In vicious purpose and malignant hope
To ape my Godhead. [*Thunder.*

### Tannhäuser.

Thunder rolls again.
I am uneasy.

### Venus.

Heed it not at all!
May not my servants of the elements
Play children's gambols on the mountain crest
About our fortress? Leave this idle talk!
Come, in this sweet abandonment of self—
Come, with this kiss I seal thy loyal oath
To spit upon her!

### Tannhäuser.

Ah, you murder me!
                    [*Sings.*]
Come, love, and kiss my shoulders! Sleepy lies
The tinted bosom whence its fire flies,
The breathing life of thee, and swoons, and sighs,
And dies!
None but the dead can know the worth of love!

Come, love, thy bosom to my heart recalls
Strange festivals and subtle funerals.
Soft passion rises in the amber walls,
And falls!
None but the dead can breathe the life of love!

48

Come, love, thy lips, curved hollow as the moon's!
Bring me thy kisses, for the seawind tunes,
    The song that soars, and reads the starry runes,
    And swoons!
    None but the dead can tune the lyre of love!

Come, love, thy body serpentine and bright!
What love is this, the heart of sombre light,
    Impossible, and therefore infinite?
    Sheer height!
    None but the dead can twine the limbs of love.

Come, love! My body in thy passion weeps
Tears keen as dewfall's, salter than the deep's.
    My bosom! How its fortress wakes, and leaps,
    And sleeps!
    None but the dead can sleep the sleep of love!

Come, love, caress me with endearing eyes!
Light the long rapture that nor fades nor flies!
    Love laughs and lingers, frenzies, stabs, and sighs,
    And dies!
    None but the dead can know the worth of love!
                      [*Tannhäuser sleeps.*]

### Venus.

Sleep on, poor fool, and in thy sleep forlorn
Defy the very beauty that thou seekest!
Now is the solemn portal of the dusk
Lifted; and in the gleaming silver-gray,
The eastern sky, steps out the single One,

Hathoör and Aphrodite—whom I mock!
I may not follow in the dimness—I
Chained unto matter by my evil will,
Delight of death and carnal life. But see!
He stirs, as one beholding in a dream
Some deadly serpent or foul basilisk
Sunning its scales, called kingly, in the mire.
Strike, O my lover! I will drag thee down
Into mine own unending pain and hate
To be one devil more upon the earth.—
Come! ye my serpents, wrap his bosom round
With your entangling leprosy! And me,
Let me assume the belovéd limber shape,
The crested head, the jewelled eyes of death,
And sinuous sinewy glitter of serpenthood,
That I may look once more into his face,
And, kissing, kill him! Thus to hold him fast,
Drawing his human spirit into mine
For strength, for life, for poison! Ah, my God!
These pangs, these torments! See! the sleeper wakes!
I am triumphant! For he reaches out
The sleepy arms, and turns the drowsy head
To catch the dew dissolving of my lip.
Wake, lover, wake! Thy Venus waits for thee!
Draw back, look, hunger!—and thy mouth is mine.

### Tannhäuser.

"Once I will shew Me waking. Destiny
Adds one illusion to thee. Yet, Oh child!
Yet will I not forsake thee; for thy soul,
Its splendid self, hath known Me. Fare thee well."

**Venus.**

What are these strange and silly words? Awake!
Wake and devour me with the dawn of love,
The dragon to eclipse this moon of mine!

**Tannhäuser.**

I sleep not. Those were Her mysterious words
As faded the great vision. And I knew
In some forgotten corner of my brain
Some desperate truth.

**Venus.**

Forget this foolishness!
    [*There cometh a shadow.*]
I am afraid, even I! What moves me thus?

**Tannhäuser.**

I saw the mighty vision as before
Forming in front of the awakening east,
All permeated with the rose of dawn,
And pale with delicate green light and shade,
Marvellous! So, you say, she is a witch
Seeking to rob or trick you of your power?

**Venus.**

I say so? No! I dare not! Oh forbear!

### Tannhäuser (starts up).

There, there She comes in waking! Hail to Thee!
I am afraid, I also, I myself!
Help! lover, Venus, mistress of my life!
I cannot bear the glory of the gaze.
No man shall look upon the face of God!
Where art thou? Save me from the scorpion!
I am—alone!

### Hathoör.

Light, Truth, arise, arise!

### Tannhäuser.

I see—I see! All blinded by the Light—
Thou art the Way, the Truth, the Life, the Love!
Thou, Whom I sought through ages of deep sleep
Forgotten when I died. There is no death:
Change alternating; and forgetfulness
Of one state in the other—easy truth
I could not understand! Oh hear me, hear!
Spare me the last illusion!—She is gone!

### Venus.

Save me, my knight! To thy sufficing arms
I cling in this distress of womanhood!

**Tannhäuser.**

Kiss me the last time.

**Venus.**

Whom have I but thee,
Thee in the ages? Barren were my bliss
And shorn my Godhead of eternal joy,
Barred from thy kiss.

**Tannhäuser.**

Call not thyself again
Goddess. I saw thee in the Presence there.
The scales are fallen, and mine eyes see clear.

**Venus.**

Then you would leave me? Serpent if I were,
My coils should press in dolorous delight
Thy straining bosom, and my kiss were death!
Death! Dost thou live, Tannhäuser? Sayest thou still:
"None but the dead can know the worth of love!"?

**Tannhäuser.**

Still. I am not in any sense estranged.
I yearn for thee in the first hour of spring,
As in the dying days of autumn. I
Would clasp thee, as a child its mother's throat,
Drinking celestial wine from that dear mouth,
Or with goodwill see poison in thy smile,

53

And die, still kissing thee, and kissed again!
This, though I saw thee crawl upon the earth,
Howl at Her presence Whom thou wouldest ape,
Thy tale reversed. I read that thunder now!
This, though I know thee. Aphrodite, no!
Nor Anael, nor Eva! Rather thou
Lilith, the woman-serpent, she who sucks
The breath of little children in their sleep,
Strangles young maidens, and presides upon
Sterile debauchery and unnatural loves.

### Venus.

Lilith! Ah lover! Thou hast known my name!

### Tannhäuser.

So; yet I love thee! Rended is the veil!
Calling thee Ugliness, I guessed aright,
Who saw, and see, all Beauty in thee still.
Only, a beauty risen out of Hell;
Death and delusion—ay, corruption's self,
Wickedness sliming into impotence,
Pleasure in putrefaction. But, in sleep,
I will put off that evil as a clout
Cast by a beggar.

### Venus.

And the sore is left.
Tannhäuser.
Oh, but this body, very consciousness!
I banish both. I cross the crimson wall—

My spirit shall reach up to and attain
That other.

**Venus.**

So Persephone must hold
Thy life divided in Her dark domain.

**Tannhäuser.**

Already I have tasted once of this
In its own lesser way. Ten years ago
I loved a maiden called Elizabeth.
A child she was, so delicate and frail,
Far, white, and lonely as the coldest star
Set beyond gaze of any eye but God's;
And, to forget her, found due somnolence
In such a warm brown bosom as thine own
Is fire and amber. Then I came away:—
I heard of knights no better horsed than I,
No better sworded, with no gift of song,
Who, caught by one ineffable desire,
Rode on by old mysterious watersheds,
Traversed strange seas, or battled with strange folk,
Held vigil in wild forests, all to seek
The vision of the Holy Grail. And I
Rode forth on that same foolish wandering;
And found a-many ventures on the way;
At last an old Egyptian; who bestowed
The magic word, which, when I had pronounced,
Called up thine evil corpse-light in the sky.
He riddled me—ah God! I see it now!
The bloody winepress? The ascending sun?

Thy dawning beauty and thine evil bed!
The double meaning! I had evil thoughts
When I pronounced it—else had She Herself,
Hathoör or Mary, risen. Misery!
Incessant mystery of the search for Truth!

**Venus.**

Search out my mystery a little while!

**Tannhäuser.**

There is a flush of passion in thine eyes,
An hunger in them; fascinate me now,
My serpent-woman, drawing out my breath
Into thy life, and mingling that in mine!
See the rich blood that mantles to my touch,
Invites the tooth to bite the shimmering skin,
Till I could watch the ripe red venom flow
Slow on the hills of amber, staining them
Its own warm purple. Look, the tender stream!

**Venus.**

Let its old sleepy fragrance lull thee now,
Yet madden thee in brain and sense and soul,
Mixing success with infinite despair.
So; take our secret back to sleep with us:—
And in that sleep I know that thou wilt choose
The fact, and leave the dream, and so disdain
These far-off splendours, catch the nearer joy,
Take squalid kisses, banish crested love
Intangible. Delights it thee, my friend,

To reach the summits unattained before,
And stumble on their snows? Thine old desire
Was just to touch the mere impalpable.
To formulate the formless. Otherwise
Christ did as well—thine own words turn again!

**Tannhäuser.**

Ah, if pure love could grow material!
There are pure women!

**Venus.**

There you make me laugh!
Remember—I have known such. But besides
You ask hot snow and leaden feather-flights!

**Tannhäuser.**

And you—you keep me worrying, fair queen,
In logic and its meshes, when to-day
I rather would be caught in other nets,
The burning gold and glory of your hair,
Lightning and sunshine, storm and radiance,
Your flaming pell!

**Venus.**

Come, sing to me again!
That we may watch each other as you sing;
Feel how it overmasters and o'erwhelms,
The growing pang of hunger for a kiss!

### Tannhäuser.

Brood evil, then, in your amazing eyes,
That I may see the serpent grow in you;
As I were just the bird upon the bough—
So let the twittering grow faint and still,
And let me fall, fall into the abyss,
Your arms—a culminating ecstasy,
Darkness and death and rapture. Sing to you?
What song? My tunes are played upon too oft.
My first great cry of love inaudible
Sapped me of music.

### Venus.

Sing me that again!

### Tannhäuser.

Who is this maiden robéd for a bride,
White shoulders and bright brows adorable,
The flaming locks that clothe her, and abide,
As God were bathing in the fire of Hell?
They change, they grow, they shake
As sunlight on the lake:
They hiss, they glisten on her bosom bare.
O maiden, maiden queen!
The lightning flows between
Thy mounting breasts, too magically fair.
Draw me, O draw me to a dreaming death!
Send out thine opiate breath,
And lull me to the everlasting sleep,
That, closing from the kisses of disdain

To ecstasy of pain,
I may sob out my life into their dangerous deep.
Who cometh from the mountain as a tower
Stalwart and set against the fiery foes?
Who, breathing as a jasmine-laden bower?
Who, crowned and lissome as a living rose?
Sharp thorns in thee are set;
In me, in me beget
The dolorous despair of this desire.
Thy body sways and swings
Above the tide of things,
Laps me as ocean, wraps me round as fire!
Ye elemental sorceries of song,
Surge, strenuous and strong,
Seeking dead dreams, the secret of the shrine;
So that she drain my life and being up
As from a golden cup,
To mingle in her blood, death's kiss incarnadine.

Who cometh from the ocean as a flower?
Who blossometh above the barren sea?
Thy lotus set beneath thee for a bower,
Thine eyes awakened, lightened, fallen on me?
O Goddess, queen, and wife!
O Lady of my life!
Who set thy stature as a wood to wave?
Whose love begat thy limbs?
Whose wave-washed body swims
That nurtured thee, and found herself a grave?
But thou, O thou, hast risen from the deep!
All mortals mourn and weep
To see thee, seeing that all love must die
Beside thy beauty, see thee and despair!

Deadly as thou art fair,
I cry for all mankind—they are slain, even as I!

[*Tannhäuser pauses, bends eagerly towards Venus.
She smiling luxuriously, he continues.*]

Who cometh wanton, with long arms outspread?
Who cometh with lascivious lips aflame?
Whose eyes invite me to the nakéd bed
Stark open to the sun, dear pride of shame?
Whose face draws close and near,
Filling the soul with fear,
Till nameless shudders course in every limb?
Whose breath is quick and fierce?
Whose teeth are keen to pierce
The arms that clasp her? Whose the eyes that swim
For dear and delicate delight? And whose
The lips that halt and choose
The very centre of my mouth, and meet
In one supreme and conquering kiss, and cleave
Unto the wound they leave,
Bringing all heart's blood to one house, too sore
and sweet?
Who rageth as a lioness bereaved,
If, for a moment's breathing space, I move
Back from the purple where her bosom heaved,
Back from the chosen body that I love?
Whose lips cling faster still
In desperate sweet will?
Whose body melts as fire caught in wine
Into the clasping soul?
Whose breathing breasts control
Her heart's quick pulsing, and the sob of mine?

O Venus, lady Venus, thou it is
Whose fierce immortal kiss
Abides upon me, about me, and within!
Thou, lady of the secret of the Sea,
Made one for love with me,
Love and desire and dream, a sense of mortal sin!

Who cometh as a visionary shape
Within my soul and spirit to abide,
Mysterious labyrinth without escape,
Magical lover, and enchanted bride?
O Mother of my will!
Set thy live body still
Unto my heart, that even Eternity
Roll by our barren bed—
That even the quick and dead,
Being mortal, mix in our eternal sea!
Distil we love from all the universe!
Defy the early curse!
Bid thorns and thistles mingle in delight!
And from the athanor of death and pain
Bring golden showers of rain
To crown our bed withal, the empire of the Night!

O Wife! Incarnate Beauty self-create!
O Life! O Death! Love unimaginable!
Despair grows hope, as hope grows desperate;
And Heaven bridges the great gulf of Hell.
Thy life is met with mine,
Transmuted, grown divine,
Even in this, the evil of the world!
What agony is this,
The first undying kiss

From jewelled eyes and lips in passion curled?
O sister and O serpent and O mate,
Strike the red fang of hate
Steady and strong, persistent to the heart!
So shall this song be made more terrible
With the soul-mastering spell,
Choke, stagger, know the Evil, Beauty's counterpart!

Whose long-drawn curse runs venom in my veins?
What dragon spouse consumes me with her breath?
What passionate hatred, what infernal pains,
Mixed with thy being in the womb of Death?
Blistering fire runs,
Scorching, terrific suns,
Through body and soul in this abominable
Marriage of demon power
Subtle and strong and sour,
A draught of ichor of the veins of Hell!
Curses leap leprous, epicene, unclean,
The soul of the Obscene
Incarnate in the spirit: and above
Hangs Sin, vast vampire, the corrupt, that swings
Her unredeeming wings
Over the world, and flaps for lust of Death—and
Love!

### Venus.

This man was drained of music!
Five new songs
Chase the three ancient to oblivion! Oh!
Love is grown fury!

**Tannhäuser.**

Kill me!

**Venus.**

In the kiss.

[*Tannhäuser sleeps.*]

# ACT III.

For Love is lord of truth and loyalty,
Lifting himself out of the lowly dust
On golden plumes up to the purest sky,
Above the reach of loathly sinful lust,
Whose base affect through cowardly distrust
Of his weak wings dare not to heaven fly,
But like a moldwarp in the earth doth lie.

His dunghill thoughts, which do themselves enure
To dirty dross, no higher dare aspire,
Nor can his feeble earthly eyes endure
The flaming light of that celestial fire
Which kindleth love in generous desire,
And makes him mount above the native might
Of heavy earth, up to the heaven's height.

SPENSER, *Hymn in Honour of Love.*

In Venusberg: changing afterward to a woodland cross-way.

### Venus.

GONE to his Goddess! the poor worm's asleep.
And yet—I cannot follow him. Not even
Into the dreamland that these mortals use.
There, I am barred. The flaming sword of Light
Is set against me, and new pangs consume
This nest of scorpions where my heart once was.
Yet to my fearful task of hate I set
No faltering bosom. I will have this man,
His life, his strength; and live a little more.
Life—shall I ever reach the splendid sword
Of womanhood, and gird it, gain my will,
A human soul, and from that altitude
Renew the terrible war against the Gods?
I have called Chronos the devouring God
My father—shall his desolating reign
Never return? Ay me! this heart of hate,
Loathing the man, takes comfort in the beast,
And gloats on the new garbage for an hour.
So, Sin, embrace me! Watch; he moves again,
Transfigured by the dream: slow rapture steals
Over his face. Mere godhead could not bring
That human light and living! I will win.
He must have banished Her—and dreams of me.

### TANNHÄUSER (*in sleep*).
Elizabeth!

### Venus.

His far-off baby-love!
I triumph, then! The Goddess hath withdrawn.

66

His mind works back to childhood, babydom,
Will grow to manhood and remember me.

TANNHÄUSER (*awaking, leaps to his feet*).

Freedom! Elizabeth! All hail to Her!
Radiant Goddess! Liberty and love!

**Venus.**

What sayest thou? Curse Her!

**Tannhäuser.**

My Elizabeth!

**Venus.**

What? Art thou mad? Come close to me again.
Forget this nightmare. Rather, tell me it,
And I will soothe thee. Have I not a balm,
A sovereign comfort in my old caress?

**Tannhäuser.**

I must begone. She waits.

**Venus.**

Who waits? Come here!
Let us talk fondly, set together still,
Not with these shouts and wavings of the arms,
Struts and unseemly gestures. Tannhäuser!

### Tannhäuser.

She waits for me, my sweet Elizabeth!
Venus or Lilith, I have loved thee well!
Now, to my freedom!

### Venus.

Your Elizabeth!

### Tannhäuser.

Ay, to those pure and alabaster brows,
The tender fingers, and the maiden smile.
Burn the whore's bed! Unpaint the cruel lips!
Cover the shameless belly, and forget
The cunning attitudes and aptitudes!
Unlearn the mowings, the lascivious grins!
I perceive purity.

### Venus.

Nay, I have loved thee!
Fresh pleasure hourly filled the crystal cup.
Shalt thou find wine so comely and so keen,
So fresh with life to fill each aching vein
With new electric fervour? Will she be
My equal? She is mortal and a child.
Her arms are frail and white. Her lily cheeks
Could never take thy kiss. Thy love would shock,
Repel. I scorn to say her love were less
Than mine: I tell thee that she could not love

Thee even at all as thou wouldst understand.

**Tannhäuser.**

So certain art thou? Let me go to her,
Try, and come back!

**Venus.**

No doubt of that success!
A child is easy to degrade!

**Tannhäuser.**

Vile thing
I will try otherwise—to raise myself:
But if I fail, I will not drag her down;
I will return.

**Venus.**

To lose thee for one hour
Is my swift death—so desolate am I!
I have not got one lover in the world,
Save only Tannhäuser. And he will go.

**Tannhäuser.**

One lover! Who makes up the equal soul
Of all the wickedness beneath the sun?
Lilith! Seek out thy children to devour!
Leave me. I go to my Elizabeth.

### Venus.

O no! It kills me! That is naked truth.
I am the soul and symbol of desire,
Yet individual to thy love. Stay! Stay!
One last caress, and then I let thee go,
And—die. I fear, and I detest, this death.
I am not mortal, doomed to it! I slip
Into mere slime; no resurrection waits
Me, made the vilest of the stars that fell.
I must not die. I dare not. But for thee,
Thy love, one last extreme delirium!—
Take thou this dagger! At the miracle
Of a moment when our lips are fastened close
Once more, in the unutterable kiss,
Drive its sharp spirit to my heart!

### Tannhäuser.

Not I!
I know the spell. I am warned. I will begone.

### Venus.

I swear I will not let thee! Thinkest thou
So long I have held thee not to have the power
To hold thee still by charm, or love, or force?
Fool, for I hate thee! I will have thy life!

### Tannhäuser.

Where is the cavern in the mountain side,
The accurséd gateway of this house of Hell?

**Venus.**

Thou canst not find it! Fool!

**Tannhäuser.**

And yet I will.

**Venus.**

Meanwhile my chant shall tremble in the air,
And rack thy limbs with poison, wither up
The fine full blood, breed serpents in thy heart,
And worms to eat thee. Living thou shalt be
A sensible corpse, a walking sepulchre.
Come, come, Apollyon! Come, my Aggereth!
Belial, cheat his ears and blind his eyes!
Come, all ye tribes of serpents and foul fish!
Beetle and worm, I have a feast for you!

**Tannhäuser.**

The palace staggers. I can hardly see—
Only these writhing horrors. I am blind!

**Venus.**

Ha! My true knight! I ask thee once again,
Once more invoke the epithets of love,
Suspend my powers—constrain thee on my knees
For thine old kisses. See, I am all thine!
All thine the splendid body, and the shape

71

Of mighty breasts, and supple limbs, and wide
Lips, and slow almond eyes! Adorable,
Seductive, sombre, moving amorously,
Droop the long eyelids, purple with young blood,
The lazy lashes and the flowing mane,
The flame of fire from head to feet of me!
The subtle fervours, drunken heats and ways,
And perfumes maddening from the soul of spring!
The little nipples, and the dangerous pit
Set smiling in the alabaster; thine,
The glowing arms are thine, the desperate
Fresh kisses, and the gold that lurks upon
The sunny skin, the marble of these brows,
The roses, and the poppies, and the scent
Subtle and sinful—thine, all thine, are these,
What with my heart that only beats for thee,
The many-throned and many-minded soul
Centred to do thee worship. Hither, hither!

#### Tannhäuser.

This shakes my spirit as a winnower
Whose fan is the eternal breath of God;
Yet on my forehead I perceive a star
That shames thy beauties and thy manifold
Mind with its tiny triple flame. I go!

#### Venus.

Try not the impossible. Thou knowest my power.
I shall renew the charm.

### Tannhäuser.

I see a Power
Above thy mockery of witchcraft. Work
Thy devilish lusts on me unfortunate!
There is no gateway to this fortalice?
Thy fiends surround me? Hein! their pangs begin!
I have one word, one cry, one exorcism:
Avé Maria!

### Venus.

Mercy! Mercy, God!

[*Thunder rolls in the lightning-riven sky. All the illusion
vanishes, and Tannhäuser finds himself in a cross-way of the
forest, where is a Crucifix. He is kneeling at the foot, amazed,
as one awakening from a dream, or from a vision of mysterious
power.*]

### Tannhäuser.

I am escapéd as a little bird
Out of the fowler's net. I thank Thee, God!
For in the pit of horror, and the clay
Of death I cried, and Thou hast holpen me,
Set me upon a rock, established me,
And filled my mouth, and tuned mine ancient lyre
With a new song—praise, praise to God above,
And to Our Lady of the Smitten Heart,
That David never knew: my pettiness
Exceeding through Her mercy and Her might
The King and Priest of Israel; for I know

Her love, and She hath shewn to me Her face,
And given me a magic star to stand
Over the house that hides Elizabeth.

[*A shepherd-boy is discovered upon a rock hard by.*]

### Shepherd-boy.

Ta-lirra-lirra! Hillo-ho! The morning!
[*He plays upon his flute.*]

### Tannhäuser.

These were the melodies that I despised!
Oh God! Be merciful to sinful me,
And keep me in the Way of Truth. But Thou!
Forgive, forgive! Lead, lead me to Thy Light!

### SHEPHERD-BOY (*sings*).

Light in the sky
Dawns to the East!
Song-bird and beast
Wake and reply.
Let me not die,
Now, at the least!
Lord of the Light!
Queen of the dawn!
Soul of the Night
Hid and withdrawn!
Voice of the thunder!
Light of the levin!
I worship and wonder,

O maker of Heaven!
The night falls asunder;
The darkness is riven!

Light, O eternal!
Life, O diurnal!
Love, O withdrawn!
Heart of my May, spring
Far to Thy dawn!
God of the dayspring!
Sun on the lawn!
Hail to Thy splendour,
Holy, I cry!
Mary shall bend her
Face from the sky,
Subtle and tender—
Then I can die!

### Tannhäuser.

The simple love of life and gladness there!
Merely to be, and worship at the heart.
How complex, the machinery of me!
Better? I doubt it. Hark! he tunes again.

### SHEPHERD-BOY (sings).

O Gretchen, when the morn is grey,
Forsake thy flocks and steal away
To that low bank where, shepherds say,
The flowers eternal are.
Thine eyes should gleam to see me there,
As fixed upon a star.

And yet thy lips should take a tune,
And match me unaware—
So steals the sun beside the moon
And hides her lustre rare.
The bloom upon the peach is fine;
The blossom on thy cheek is mine!
O kiss me—if you dare!
I called thee by the name of love
That mothers fear and gods approve,
And maidens blush to say—
O Gretchen, meet me in the dell
We know and love, who love so well,
While morn is cold and gray!
So, match thy blushes to the dawn;
Thy bosom to the rising moon,
Until our loves to earth have drawn
Some new bewitching tune.
Come, Gretchen, in the dusk of day,
Where nymphs and dryads creep away
Beneath the oaks, to laugh and play
And sink in lover's swoon.
We'll sing them sister songs, and shew
What secrets mortal lovers know.

### Tannhäuser.

The simple life of love and joy therein!
Merely to love—to take such pride in it
Gods must behold! The childish easiness,
Impossible to me, who am become
Perhaps the subtlest mind of men. Alas!
Maybe in this I still am self-deceived,
Merely the fool swelled up with bitter words,

Imagination, and the toadstool growth,
Thought, wounded; as a scorpion to sting
Its own bruised life out. This is Tannhäuser!
How long ago since he took pleasure in
Such love—                    [*A horn winds.*]
such music as yon horn below—

[*A chant is heard.*]

Such worship as the simple chant that steals
Calm and majestic in the solitude
Up from the valley. Pilgrims, by my fay!

[*Enter* PILGRIMS.]

### Pilgrims.

Hail to Thee, Lady bright,
Queen of the stars of night!
Avé Maria!
Spouse of the Breath divine,
Hail to Thee, shrouded shrine,
Whence our Redeemer came!
Hail to Thy holy name!
Avé Maria!

### Tannhäuser.

Those words that saved me!

### Shepherd-boy.

Pray, your blessing, sirs!
I worship Mary in my simple way,
And see Her name in all the starry host,
And Jesus crucified on every tree

77

For me! God speed you to the House of God!

### The Eldest Pilgrim.

The Blessing of the Virgin on your head!

### The Youngest Pilgrim.

What make you, sir, so downcast? Come with us
Who taste all happiness in uneasiness,
Hunger and thirst, in His sweet Name—

### Tannhäuser.

Ah no!
I have been shown another way than yours!
I am too old in this world's weariness,
Too hungry in its hunger unto God,
Too foolish-wise, too passionate-cynical,
To seek your royal road to Deity!

### Another Pilgrim.

Leave him! Belike 'tis some philosopher
With words too big to understand himself.

### Tannhäuser.

With heart too seared to understand himself!
With mind too wise to understand himself!
With soul too small to understand himself!

### Eldest Pilgrim.

Cling to the Cross, sir, there is hope in that!

### Tannhäuser.

You know not, friend, the man to whom you speak.
I have lived long in miracles enough,
Myself the crowning miracle of all,
That I am merely here. God speed you, sirs!
I ask your blessing, not to stay therewith
My soul's own need (though that is dire enough)
But—he that blesseth shall himself be blessed!
My blessing were small help to you, my friends.

### An Intelligent Pilgrim.

For your own reason, give it to us, then!

### Tannhäuser.

The Blessing of the Lord! May Mary's self
Be with you and defend you evermore,
Most from the fearful destiny of him
Men used to call the minstrel Tannhäuser!

### Eldest Pilgrim.

A sombre blessing! May God's mercy fall
On you and yours!

### Tannhäuser.

On mine, ah mine! Amen
Amen to that!

### ELDEST PILGRIM (*smiles*).

On her you love, my friend!
We will pass onward, by your honour's leave!

### Pilgrims.

Hail, hail, O Queen, to Thee,
Spouse of Eternity!
Avé Maria!
Mother in Maidenhood!
Saintly Beatitude!
Queen of the Angel Host!
Bride of the Holy Ghost!
Avé Maria!              [*Exeunt Pilgrims.*]

### Tannhäuser.

The love of Isis! No mere love to Her
That is inborn in every soul of us!
It is Her love to Christ that we must taste,
Uniting us with Her eternal sigh.
There is a problem infinite again.
I have not gained one jot since first I saw
The stately bosom of the Venusberg,
Save that mine eyes have seen a little truth,
My body found a little weariness.
I am very feeble! Hither comes the hunt!

[*A horn winds quite close by.*]
The noble, doomed, swift beauty! Closer yet
Pant the long hounds! What heart he has! One, two!
See the brach dying by his bloody flank!
So could not Tannhäuser awhile ago.
My help lay outside and above myself.
What skills him he is brave? He ends the same.
Poor stag! Here sweep the foremost hunters up.
My very kinsmen! There rides Wolfram too!
The proper minstrel! The ideal lover!
The pure, unsullied soul. Even so, forsooth!
They tell no secrets in the scullery.
And there is Heinrich, wastrel of the Court,
Yet hides a heart beneath the foolish face.
And lo! The Landgrave! Flushed, undignified!
The chase was long—if he could see himself!
Wind, wind the mort! What call will answer me
When I step forward? Am I dead, I wonder,
Or merely on my hare-brain quest? Three years
Since I was seen in Germany!
    [*He descends the hill and enters the company.*]
Hail, friends!
Good cousin Landgrave, merry be the meet!

### Landgrave.

Hands off me, fellow!   Who are you?

### Tannhäuser.

My lord,
Your cousin. Is my face so changed with care,
My body shrunken with my suffering

81

(That was not ever of the body) so?

**Wolfram.**

I know you, my old friend! Our chiefest bird!
Sweetest of singers!

**Tannhäuser.**

No, the naughty one!

Heinrich.

Tannhäuser! Yes! And we have thought you dead.

**Landgrave.**

Friends, will you swear to him?

**Heinrich.**

Yes, yes, 'tis he!

**Wolfram.**

I know the blithe look in the sober eyes!

**Landgrave.**

Changed verily. It was most urgent, cousin,
I were assured of your identity.
Three weeks the couriers scour the land for you,
Urgent demands:—how came you here at last?

Your horse? Your arms? Three years since Germany
Saw the brave eyes and kindly face of you!
Where have you been? Upon the sacred quest
Still riding?

**Tannhäuser.**

Ay, my lord, upon the quest.

**Landgrave.**

You travelled in far lands?

**Tannhäuser.**

Far, very far!

**Landgrave.**

You fought with Turks?

**Tannhäuser.**

I fought within myself.

**Landgrave.**

Why is such suffering written in dark lines,
And painted in the greyness of your hair?

**Tannhäuser.**

I had an evil dream.

**Landgrave.**

You saw the Grail?

**Tannhäuser.**

I saw—strange things.

**Wolfram.**

For very feebleness
Your limbs shake under you. How hither, friend?
Your horse and arms? Your squire?

TANNHÄUSER (*with sudden passion*).

My squire is dead.
I am no weakling that I need a knave
Hanging upon me—'tis an incubus.

**Landgrave.**

And then your horse?

**Tannhäuser.**

I know not; possibly
Kept as an hostage.    I was prisoner once.

**Wolfram.**

Prisoner? By here?

**Tannhäuser.**

A-many castles, sir,
Held by old ogres—and not all of them
Stand in the mid-day, front the sober sun,
Answer the slug-horn.

**Landgrave.**

You are pleased to riddle.
Ever the poet!

TANNHÄUSER (*aside*).

Let me try the truth
For certitude of incredulity!
(*Aloud, laughing*) I was in Venusberg!
        ALL (*EXCEPT* HEINRICH, *WHO LAUGHS*).
Save us, Maria!
    [*They look about them fearfully and cross them-selves.*]

**Landgrave.**

Even in jest, such words!—Most dangerous
Even to think of!—but to speak!

HEINRICH (*aside*).

These fools!
[*He remains, thoughtfully regarding Tannhäuser.*]

**Landgrave.**

God avert omens! Soft you, Tannhäuser,
You heard the heralds?

**Tannhäuser.**

Never a word of them!

**Landgrave.**

You must remember my Elizabeth,
My daughter—I designed to marry her
To a most noble youth—

**Tannhäuser.**

Von Aschenheim?

**Landgrave.**

The same. I would have wed her, but ('tis strange!)
The lady had a purpose of her own,
And swore by all the Virgins in the Book
She would wed nobody but—Tannhäuser.
So, like the foolish, doting sire I am,
I gave her thirty days to find you. This
Must dumb you with astonishment.

**Tannhäuser.**

Well, no!

The details, unfamiliar! But the theme
I knew. And therefore leaps my bosom up:
I rob your verderer of his nag, and ho!
Low the long gallop to Elizabeth!

### Wolfram.

Lucky and brave.   How we all envy you!

### Heinrich.

Envy?   This day when he comes back to us!
Why, we are lucky too! We thought you dead!

### Wolfram.

Begrudge you, no! But—wish our luck were yours?
Yes! Come, Tannhäuser, there's my hand on it!
Luck, love, and loyalty—the triple toast!

### Foresters.

Tannhäuser! Luck, and love, and loyalty!

### Tannhäuser.

I thank you, loving kinsmen and my friends.
But see, I am impatient to be gone!
Your horse—that favour I shall not forget,
Nor linger to repay. Good morrow then!
Good sport all day!

### Landgrave.

God speed thee, Tannhäuser.

[Exit Tannhäuser.]

Am I still dreaming? It was surely he
But such an one, compact of suffering,
Of joy, of love, of pity, of despair;
Half senseless, half too subtle for my sense.

### Wolfram.

He has passed through some unimagined test,
Or undergone some sorrow. Leave it so!
I saw high grief upon him, and new love!

### Heinrich.

You are the poet! To your instinct then!
Here's to the insight given us by God!

### Landgrave.

Wolfram is right; a truce to jest to-day.
The dogs are loose. Ride forward, gentlemen!

[*Amid the winding of horns and cries of the*
huntsmen the company moves off.

### Heinrich.

They hate his very name! Dear Tannhäuser!

[Exit.]

# ACT IV.

"So, force is sorrow, and each sorrow, force:
What then? since Swiftness gives the charioteer
The palm, his hope be in the vivid horse
Whose neck God clothed with thunder, not the steer
Sluggish and safe! Yoke Hatred, Crime, Remorse,
Despair: but ever mind the whirling fear,
Let, through the tumult, break the poet's face
Radiant, assured his wild slaves win the race!"

Two Poets of Croisic.

## SCENE I.

A room in the palace of the Landgrave.

**Elizabeth.**

I AM ashamed to look upon thy face!

### Tannhäuser.

O Love! Pure mystery of life!

### Elizabeth.

Not so.
Learn how this came. My father would have made
A match of lands and titles. I declined,
Minded to keep my high virginity.
He laughed, was cruel. So I said at last:
"Tannhäuser only!" Was this modesty?
Listen. You loved me when I was a child;
And, in my childish way, I looked to you,
Loved sitting at your knee and toying with
The great cross-hilt, or watching how the steel
Outshone the jewelled scabbard when you drew
(You would not let me touch) the delicate blade
Half out: and also fingering your harp,
Picking child's tunes out, while you curled my hair
Between two fingers, dreamily enough!
Then, too, you went away out of my life!
You see the symbol you have been to me?
The swift high mind, the heart of gold and fire,
The living purpose and the mystic life
Of lonely seeking for the Grail of God!
I—call you husband? When I said your name,
It was to set the task impossible:—
Had they but known it—just as one should say:
"Bring down St Michael: let me marry him!"
They knew the angels were too pure; but you,
They guessed not how exalted were your hopes;
How utterly unselfish, pure, and true,

Your great heart beat!

TANNHÄUSER (*with bitterness*).

I hardly knew, myself!
(*Aside.*)   Here is the virgin insight of the truth!
Or—cannot purity be brought to know
Aught but itself? Some poets tell us that!
(*Aloud.*)   I am unworthy even to speak to you.

**Elizabeth.**

The proof!   The proof!   Dear God, how true it is
That such high worthiness sees nothing there
In his own heart (save what is very Christ)
But wickedness!

TANNHÄUSER (*aside*).

This is my punishment!
This faith, this hope, this love—to me—to me!

**Elizabeth.**

Yet, once my word went forth into the world.
Suddenly came the fear that you were still
Accessible to men—might hear, might come!
The kind, grave face of you—that light outshone
The mystical ideal. Therefore too
I minded me of our old baby-love,
And—marriages are made in heaven, you know!
Besides—Our Lady shewed me in a dream
How you would come.

### Tannhäuser.

And now? So sure are you
The loving word you spoke an hour ago
Came from the heart—who called me by mistake?

### Elizabeth.

So sure? You want me to confess again
The deep pure love, the love indicible.

### TANNHÄUSER (*to himself*).
Words, thoughts, that fail her? How should acts exceed?

(*Aloud.*)   Better sit thus and read each other's thoughts—
I in the blue eyes, in the hazel you!
Then, bending, I may touch my lips upon
Sweet thoughtful brows.

### Elizabeth.

Your kisses move my soul.
Strange thoughts and unimagined destinies
Take ship, and harbour in the heart of me.

### Tannhäuser.

Words mean too much, and never mean enough.
Look, only look!

#### Elizabeth.

I am so happy—so!

# SCENE II.

The Court assembled in the Great Hall. Landgrave enthroned, Elizabeth by his side. Facing them are the competing minstrels. Around, courtiers and fair ladies.

#### Landgrave.

Welcome all minstrels! Let us celebrate
In the old fashion, dear to Germany,
My child's betrothal to this noble youth,
Great lord, true knight, and honest gentleman,
So long who journeyed on the holy quest
Forgotten of these younger days, and now
Come back among us to receive reward
For those long sufferings; in days of peace,
In fruitful love, and marriage happiness.
So, to the poet's tourney.

#### Wolfram.

Sire, Lord Heinrich
Craves your high pardon.

### Landgrave.

Ha! He is not here!

### Wolfram.

Our sturdy lover will not be consoled
For losing, as he phrases it, his friend.

### Landgrave.

Well, we forgive him the more readily
Because of the occasion. One alone
Of all themes possible may grace this hour;—
Love! Let the lots of precedence be drawn.
Tannhäuser, you will string us once again
Your harp forgotten?

### Tannhäuser.

That will I, my lord.

### Herald.

On the Lord Wolfram falls it first to sing.

### WOLFRAM (*sings*).

Tender the smile, and faint the lover's sigh,
When first love dawns in the blue maiden sky,
Where happy peace is linked with purity.

As sad spring's sun starts on his daily race,

Reddens the east, as if in sad disgrace;
So love first blushes on a true maiden's face.

Soft, soft, the gaze of married folk, I think,
Limpid and calm as pools where cattle drink;
And, when they kiss, most discontentments shrink!

Even as the stars together sing (we hear)
So sings the married life, a tuneful sphere.
Husband is he, and she is very dear.

How truly beautiful it is to see
Old age in perfect unanimity,
Affections smooth, and buzzing like a bee.

The sun sets, in conjunction with the moon.
Death comes at last, a pleasure and a boon,
And they arrive in heaven very soon.

[*Immense, spontaneous, uncontrollable applause*
sweeps like a whirlwind through the court.

AN UNKNOWN MINSTREL (*breaking in unheralded*).
Tender the phrase, and faint the melody,
When poets praise a maiden's purity;
Platitude linked to imbecility.
                              [*Murmurs of surprise.*]
   As 'mongst spring's sprigs sprouts sunshine's con-
stant face;
   Or as a mill grinds on, with steady pace;
   So sprouts, so grinds, the unblushing commonplace.

Soft, soft the brain—

[*The murmurs break into an indignant uproar.*]

### Herald.

Silence!

### Landgrave.

Sir Minstrel, you are insolent!
We do not know you, yet have borne with you,
Rudely uprising ere your turn was come:—
And you abuse our patience to insult
The noble minstrel whose impassioned song
Touched every heart. Sing in your turn you may.
Love is the theme, not imbecility!

### Wolfram.

That is the subject next his heart, no doubt!
            [*Laughter.*]

### Herald.

Lord Bertram!

### Bertram.

I shall sing in other key.
            [*Sings.*]
He is the equal of the gods, my queen,
He crowned and chosen out of men,
Who sits beside thee, sees
Love's laughing ecstasies

Flame in thy face, and alter then
To the low light of passion dimly seen
In shaded woods and dells, Love's wide demesne.

But me! I burn with love! My lips are wan!
Thy face is turned—I flame! I melt! I fall!
My heart is chilled and dark;
My soul's ethereal spark
Is dulled for sorrow; my despairs recall
At last Thy name, O gracious Paphian,
Lady of Mercy to the love of man!

Come, come, immortal, of the many thrones!
Sparrows and doves in chariot diamonded
Drawn through the midmost air!
O Lady of despair,
Who bound the golden helmet of Thy head?
Whose voice rings out the pitiful low tones:
"Who, who hath wronged thee? And my power
atones."

"She who now doth flee, shall soon pursue thee;
She who spurns thy gifts, with gifts shall woo thee;
She who loves not, she shall cleave unto thee,
Thou the unwilling!"

Peer of Gods is he, equal soul to theirs,
Who lingers in thy passionate embrace:
Whose languor-laden kiss
Cleaves where thy bosom is
A throne of beauty for thy throat and face!
In these dark joys and exquisite despairs,
O Love, let Death lay finger unawares!

**Landgrave.**

Passion and music—but no Principle!
How different is Tannhäuser!
(*To the unknown minstrel*) You, sir, next!
Sing of pure love and noble womanhood.
Our court loves not these wastrel troubadours,
Loose locks, Hushed faces, soul's unseemliness.

**THE UNKNOWN MINSTREL (*sings*).**

Amid earth's motley, Gaia's cap and bells,
This too material, too unreal life,
Sing, sing the crown of tender miracles,
The pure true wife!

Sing not of love, the unutterable one,
The love divine that Mary has to men.
Seek not the winepress and the rising sun
Beyond thy ken!

**TANNHÄUSER (*aside*).**

Who is this man that reads my inmost thought?

**The Unknown Minstrel.**

I sing of love, most delicate and pure,
Surely the crown of life! How slow and sweet
Its music! Shall the ecstasy endure,
Sunshine on wheat?

Where leads this gentle love? I see you sigh!
The Scythe is laid unto the Golden Grain:
A note of utter unreality
Usurps the strain.

I sing not of that other flame of hell
Wrapping with torture the delighted brow—
But thou! who knowest, and hast known, so well,
Sing thou!

[*Tannhäuser, entranced, imagines himself
to be still in Venusberg.*]


TANNHÄUSER (*aside*).

I have been dreaming that I left this place,
Escaped with life, wooed my Elizabeth;
My dreams are always strange in Venusberg.

[*Taking his harp.*]

Sing thee again, dear lady, of our joy?
Listen, then, listen! For some sombre finger,
Other than mine, impulses on the string.
This tune I knew not! See, the strings are moved
Subtly as if by witchcraft—or by God!

[*Sings.*]

In the Beginning God began,
And saw the Night of Time begin!
Chaos, a speck; and space, a span;
Ruinous cycles fallen in,
And Darkness on the Deep of Time.
Murmurous voices call and climb;
Faces, half-formed, arise; and He
Looked from the shadow of His throne,
The curtain of Eternity;

He looked—and saw Himself alone,
And on the sombre sea, the primal one,
Faint faces, that might not abide;
Flicker, and are foredone.
So were they caught within the spacious tide,
The sleepy waters that encased the world.
Monsters rose up, and turned themselves, and curled
Into the deep again.

The darkness brooded, and the bitter pain
Of chaos twisted the vast limbs of time
In horrid rackings: then the spasm came:
The Serpent rose, the servant of the slime,
In one dark miracle of flame
Unluminous and void: the silent claim
Of that which was, to be: the cry to climb,
The bitter birth of Nature: uttermost Night
Dwelt, inaccessible to sound and sight;
Shielded from Voice, impervious to Light.

Lo! on the barren bosom, on the brine,
The spirit of the Mighty One arose,
A flickering light, a formless triple flame,
The self-begotten, the impassive shrine,
The seat of Heaven's archipelagoes;
Yet lighted not the glory whence it came,
Nor shone upon the surface of the sea.
Time, and the Great One, and the Nameless Name,
Held in their grip the child, Eternity.
Silence and Darkness in their womb withheld
That spiritual fire, and brooded still:
Nature and Time, their soleness undispelled,

Ever awaiting the eternal Will.
And Law was unbegotten: uttermost Night
Dwelt, inaccessible to sound and sight;
Shielded from Voice, impervious to Light.

Then grew within the barren womb of this
The Breath of the Eternal and the Vast,
Softer than dawn, and closer than a kiss—
And lo! the chaos and the darkness passed!
At the creative sigh the Light became.
Chaos rolled back in the abundant flame.
The vast and mystic Soul,
The Firmament, a living coal,
Flamed 'twixt the glory and the sea below.
The whirling force began. The atom whirled
In vortices of flashing matter: wild as snow
On mountain tops by the wind-spirits hurled,
Blinding and blind, the sparks of spirit curled
Each to its proper soul; the wide wheels flow,
Orderly streams, and lose the rushing speed,
Meet, mingle, marry. Fire and air express
Their dews and winds of molten loveliness,
Fine flakes of arrowy light, the dawn's first deed.
Metallic showers and smoke self-glittering
For many an aeon. Wild the pennons spring
Of streaming flame! Then, surging from the tide,
Grew the desirable, the golden one,
Separate from the sun.
Now fire and air no more exult, exceed,
Are balanced in the sphere. The waters wide
Glow on the bosom of fixed earth; and Need,
The Lady of Beginning, also was.
Thus was the firmament a vital glass,

The waters as the vessel of the soul;
Thus earth, the mystic basis of the whole,
Was smitten through with fire, as chrysopras,
Blending, uniting, and dividing it,
Volcanic, airy, and celestial.

I rose within the elemental ball,
And lo! the Ancient One of Days did sit!
His head and hair were white as wool, His eyes
A flaming fire: and from the splendid mouth
Flashed the Eternal Sword!
Lo! Lying at his feet as dead, I saw
The leaping-forth of Law:
Division of the North wind and the South,
The lightning of the armies of the Lord;
East rolled asunder from the rended West;
Height clove the depth: the Voice begotten said:
"Divided be thy ways and limited!"
Answered the reflux and the indrawn breath:
"Let there be Life, and Death!"

"The Earth, she shall be governed by her parts:
Division be upon her! Let her glory
From crown to valley, source and spring to mouth,
North unto South,
Smooth gulf and sea to rugged promontory,
Always be vexed and drunken, that the hearts
Ruling her course round alway in the sky;
And as an handmaid let her serve and die!
One season, let it still confound another;
No man behold his brother;
No creature in it or upon, the same!
Her members, let them differ; be no soul

Equal! Let thought, let reasonable things,
Bow to thy wings,
Thy manifest control,
Vexation! weeding out of one another.
Their dwelling-places, let them lose their name!
The work of man, and all his pomp and power,
Deface them: shatter the aspiring tower!
Let all his houses be as caves and holes,
Unto the Beast I give them. And their souls—
Lift up the shadowy hand!—
Confound with darkness them that understand!
For why?
Me, the Most High,
It doth repent Me, having made mankind!
Let her be known a little while, and then
A little while a stranger. Dumb and blind,
Deaf to the Light and Breath of Me be men!
She is become an harlot's bed, the home
And dwelling of the fallen one! Arise!
Ye heavens, ye lower serving skies!
Beneath My dome
Serve ye the lofty ones. The Governors,
Them shall ye govern. Cast the fallen down!
Bring forth with them that are Fertility's!
Destroy the rotten! Let no shores
Remain in any number! Add and crown,
Diminish and discrown, until the stars
Be numbered! Rise, ye adamantine bars!
Let pass your Masters! Move ye and appear!
Execute judgment and eternal ill,
The law of justice, and the law of fear.
It is My Will!"
So shed the primal curse

Its dreadful stature, its appalling shape.
In giant horror the clouds rolling drape
Earth, like a plumed pall upon an hearse,
Till God looms up, half devil and half ape,
Heaven exulting in the hateful rape;
And still the strong curse rolls
Over accurséd and immortal souls,
Covering the corners of the universe
Without escape.

This is the evil destiny of man:
The desperate plan
Made by the Ancient One, to keep His power.
Limits He set, made space unsearchable
Yet bounded, made time endless to transcend
Man's thought to comprehend:
Builded the Tower
Of life, and girded it with walls of hell,
The name of Death. This limit in all things
Baffles the spirit wings,
Chains the swift soul; for even Death is bound.
In its apparent amplitude I saw,
I, who have slept through death, have surely found
The old accurséd law,
And death has changed to life. This task alone
Shoots to the starry throne:
That if man lack not purpose, but succeed,
Reaching in very deed
Impersonal existence;—Lo!
Man is made one with God, an equal soul.
For he shall know
The harmony, the oneness of the Whole.

This was my purpose. Vain,
Ah vain! The Star of the Unconquered Will
Centred its vehemence and light, to stain
In one successful strain,
The stainless sphere of the unchangeable,
With its own passionate, desperate breath
Ever confronting the dark gate of Death.
I passed that gate! O pitiful! The same
Mystery holds me, and the flame
Of Life stands up, unbroken citadel,
Beyond my sight, vague, far, intangible.
Broken are will, and witchery, and prayer.
Remains the life of earth, which is but hell,
Destiny's web, and my immense despair.

**Landgrave.**

Your words are terrible! We knew them true
Even while you sang. But see! the light of day!
Beauty in all things and—for you—true love!
All the blind horror of the song recedes.
There is a sequel; is there not, my friend?
Of love, your theme, we have not heard a note.

**Tannhäuser.**

That is a question. I am not so sure
My song was not entirely to that end.

**Wolfram.**

Yes, poet, true one that you are indeed!
You shew us the dilemma of the soul,

The Gordian knot Love only hews asunder.

### Tannhäuser.

Or—shall I say?—soothes only, bandages,
Not heals the sore of Destiny?

### Wolfram.

No, certes,
But substitutes for one reality
Another—and a lovely pleasant one.

### Tannhäuser.

Existence is illusion after all;
Man, a bad joke; and God, mere epigram!
If we must come to that. And likewise love.

### Landgrave.

You have dipped somewhat in philosophy
Of a too cynical and wordy sort.

### Tannhäuser.

To logic there is one reality,
Words. But the commonsense of humankind
By logic baffles logic, chains with Deed
The lion Thought. It is a circle, friends!
All life and death and mystery ravel out
Into one argument—the rounded one.

**The Unknown Minstrel.**

Count me your children their arithmetic!
Zero, the circle, grows to one, the line:
Both limitless in their own way. Proceed.
Two is by shape the Coptic aspirate,
Life breathed, and death indrawn. And so
Rounds you at last the ten, completion's self,
The circle and the line. Why stick at nought?

**Bertram.**

Only a donkey fastened to a post
Moves in a circle.

**Landgrave.**

This is noble talk!

**The Unknown Minstrel.**

Leave the wide circle—word and argument!
Move to the line—the steady will of man,
That shall attract the Two, the Breath of Life,
The Holy Spirit: land you in the Three,
Where form is perfect—in the triangle.

**Tannhäuser.**

My friend, the Three is infinitely small,
Mere surface. And I seek the Depth divine!

**The Unknown Minstrel.**

The solid! But the triangle aspires
To that same unity that you despise,
And lo! the Pyramid! The Sages say:
Unite that to the Sphinx, and all is done,
Completion of the Magnum Opus.

**Tannhäuser.**

No!
Each new dimension lands me farther yet
In the morass of limit.

**The Unknown Minstrel.**

Be it so!
But follow me through all the labyrinth,
And ten rewards us. And your Zero's found
To have an actual value and effect
On unity—your Will.

**Tannhäuser.**

What's then to seek?

**The Unknown Minstrel.**

The fourth dimension, for the early step.

**Landgrave.**

It seems this talk is merely mystical.
This is no College of the Holy Ghost
For Rosencreutz his mystifying crew!

**A Courtier.**

A Poet's tourney, and the theme is Love!

**The Unknown Minstrel.**

There is a sequel to our poet's song,
And he will sing it.

**Tannhäuser.**

No! I know it not!

**The Unknown Minstrel.**

The winepress and the sun!

TANNHÄUSER (*again in Venusberg*).

My spouse and Queen,
Bright Goddess of the amber limbs, the lips
Redder than poppies in the golden corn
That is your mane! Listen, the after-song!
                    [*Taking his harp.*]

### Landgrave.

What are these words?

### The Unknown Minstrel.

Let silence now abide:
Disturb not the impassioned utterance!

### Tannhäuser.

[*Sings.*]
Can you believe the deadly will's decree,
The bitter earnestness of this desire,
The deep intention, the solemnity,
Profound as night and penetrant as fire,
The awful grasping at the Infinite,
Even as I grapple at the breasts of thee,
The seeking and the striving to the light
Deep in thine eyes, where Hell flames steadily?
I am not clinging thus
Despairing to the body of thy sin
For mere delight—Ah, deadly is to us
The pleasure wrapping us, and holding in
All love, all hate—the miserable way!
Dawns no devouring day
Still on the infinite slow tune of limbs
Moving in rapture; sleepy echo swims
In the dissolving brain.
Love conquering lassitude at last to win
Pain out of peace, and pleasure from a pang;
Then, scorpion-stung of its own terrible tang,

Burnt of its own fire, soiled of its own stain,
Falls conquered as a bird
Bolt-stricken through the brain,
To the resounding plain:
The double word,
The see-saw of all misery—begin
The alluring mysteries of lust and sin;
Ends their delight!—and are they clear to sight?
Or mixed with death, compact of night?
Begin—the bitter tears of impotence,
The sad permuted sense
Of this despair—what would you? and renew
The long soft warfare—the enchanted arms,
The silken body's charms,
The lips that murmur and the breasts that sting
The eyes that sink so deep
Beyond the steeps and avenues of sleep,
And of their wonder bring
No ultimation from the halls of night,
The slippery staircase, and the Fatal Throne,
The Evil Mouse, the Fugitive of Light,
The great Unluminous, the Formless One!
Stoop not! Beneath, a precipice is set,
The Seven Steps. Stoop not, forget
Never the splendid Image, and the realm
Where lightnings overwhelm
The evil, and the barren, and the vile,
In God's undying smile!
Stoop not, O stoop not, to yon splendid world,
Yon darkly-splendid, airless, void, inane,
Blind confines in stupendous horror curled,
The sleepless place of Terror and distress,
Luring damned souls with lying loveliness,

The Habitation and the House of Pain.
For that is their abode, the Wretched Ones,
Of all unhappiness the sons!

And when, invoking often, thou shalt see
That formless Fire; when all the earth is shaken,
The stars abide not, and the moon is gone,
All Time crushed back into Eternity,
The Universe by earthquake overtaken;
Light is not, and the thunders roll,
The World is done:
When in the darkness Chaos rolls again
In the excited brain:
Then, O then call not to thy view that visible
Image of Nature; fatal is her name!
It fitteth not thy body to behold
That living light of Hell,
The unluminous, dead flame,
Until that body from the crucible
Hath passed, pure gold!
For, from the confines of material space,
The twilight-moving place,
The gates of matter, and the dark threshold,
Before the faces of the Things that dwell
In the Abodes of Night,
Spring into sight
Demons dog-faced, that show no mortal sign
Of Truth, but desecrate the Light Divine,
Seducing from the sacred mysteries.

But, after all these Folk of Fear are driven
Before the avenging levin
That rives the opening skies,

Behold that Formless and that Holy Flame
That hath no name;
That Fire that darts and flashes, writhes and creeps
Snake-wise in royal robe,
Wound round that vanished glory of the globe,
Unto that sky beyond the starry deeps,
Beyond the Toils of Time—then formulate
In thine own mind, luminous, concentrate,
The Lion of the Light, a child that stands
On the vast shoulders of the Steed of God:
Or winged, or shooting flying shafts, or shod
With the flame-sandals. Then, lift up thine hands!
Centre thee in thine heart one scarlet thought
Limpid with brilliance of the Light above!
Draw into nought
All life, death, hatred, love:
All self concentred in the sole desire—
Hear thou the Voice of Fire!

This hope was Zoroaster's—this is mine!
Not one but many splendours hath the Shrine:
Not one but many paths approach the gate
That guards the Adytum, fortifying Fate!
Mine was, by weariness of blood and brain,
Mere bitter fruit of pain
Sought in the darkness of an harlot's bed,
To make me as one dead:
To loose the girders of the soul, and gain
Breathing and life for the Intelligible;
Find death, yet find it living. Deep as Hell
I plunged the soul; by all blind Heaven unbound
The spirit, freed, pierced through the maze profound,

And knew Itself, an eagle for a dove.
So in one man the height and deep of love
Joined, in two states alternate (even so
Are life and death)—shall one unite the two,
My long impulsive strife?
Did I find life?
The real life—to know
The ways of God. Alas! I never knew.
Then came our Lady of the Sevenfold Light,
Shewed me a distant plan, distinct and clear,
As twilight to the dayspring and the night,
Dividing and uniting even here:
The middle path—life interfused with death—
Pure love; the secret of Elizabeth!
This is my secret—in the man's delight
To lose that stubborn ecstasy for God!
To this clear knowledge hath my path been trod
In deepest hell—in the profoundest sky!
This knowledge—the true immortality,
I came unto through pain and tears,
Tigerish hopes, and serpent loves, and dragon fears,
Most bitter kisses, salted springs and dry;
In those deep caverns and slow-moving years,
When dwelt I, in the Mount of Venus, even I!
        [*The spell is broken, and uproar ensues.*]


## Landgrave.

The fiend! The atheist! Devil that you are!


## Voices.

Kill him, ay, kill him!

### Tannhäuser.

Crucify him, say!
[*Tannhäuser extends his arms as on a cross.*]

### Landgrave.

Blaspheme not! Dare not to insult the sign
Of our Redemption! Gentlemen and peers,
What say you? shall he live to boast himself,
The abandoned, perjured, the apostate soul,
Daring to come to our pure court to brag
Of his incredible vileness? To link up
The saintly purity of this my child
With his seducer's heart of hell!    My voice!
Death! Your cry echoes me?

### Voices.

Death! Death!

### Tannhäuser.

Leap out,
Sword of my fathers! you have heard my harp!
Its music stings your vile hypocrisy
Into mere hatred. Truth is terrible!
You, cousin, taken in adultery!
You, Wolfram, lover of the kitchen maids!
You, Jerome—yes, I know your secret deeds!
You, ladies! Are your faces painted thus
Not to hide wrinkles of debauchery?

115

To catch new lovers?

### Landgrave.

Stop the lying mouth!
Friends, your sword-service!

### Tannhäuser.

Will they answer you?
My arm is weary as your souls are not
Of beastliness: I have drawn my father's sword,
Hard as your virtue is the easy sort,
Heavy to handle as your loves are light,
Smooth as your lies, and sharper than your hates!
I know you! Cowards to the very bone!
                    [*Driving them out.*]
Who fights me, of this sworded company?
Cannot my words have sting in them enough,
Now, to make one of you turn suddenly
And stab me from behind? Out, out with you!
Fling-to the doors! A murrain on the curs!
So, I am master!

### The Unknown Minstrel.

Well and merrily done!
But look you to the lady; she has swooned.

### Tannhäuser.

Who are you, sir, stood smiling, nonchalant,
At all the turmoil, ridiculing it?

You knew the secret symbol of my life,
You forced me to that miserable song.

**The Unknown Minstrel.**

My name, sir, at your service, is GESCHICHT.

**Tannhäuser.**

Sent? And the purpose of your coming here?
You must wield power to keep them silent so,
When the first word had culminated else
In twice the tempest echoed to the last!

**The Unknown Minstrel.**

It was most necessary for yourself
To formulate your thought in word.   Enough—
The thought transmuted in the very act.

**Tannhäuser.**

You know? You know! The new illusion gone!
Bitter, O bitter will it be to say!

**The Unknown Minstrel.**

Due grace and courage will be found for you.
Farewell, Tannhäuser!

**Tannhäuser.**

Shall we meet again?

### The Unknown Minstrel.

There is one glamour you must wreathe in gloom
Before you come to the dark hill of dreams.

### Tannhäuser.

My soul is sick of riddling. Fare you well!
                    [*Exit the Unknown Minstrel.*]
Wake, wake, poor child, poor child, Elizabeth!

### Elizabeth.

What says my dear one?    I have been with God.

### TANNHÄUSER (*aside*).

How shall I speak? A violent good-bye,
As one distraught, ashamed? I had unbared
My bosom to these folk, but the sole pride,
My father's gift—to be a gentleman—
Forbade the dying, welcome otherwise,
At any despicable hands as theirs.
They, they might boast—we hundred swords or so
Set on the mighty Tannhäuser, and slew him.
We, scarce an hundred! Yes, believe it, sirs
We are not so feeble!—But death anyhow
Cuts and not loosens the entangled life.
Be mine the harder and the better way,
The single chance: not hope; appeal no more;
Hardly the arrowy wisdom of despair;

Hardly the cowardice or courage yet
To drift, nor cursing nor invoking God.

### Elizabeth.

I heard, I pure, I virginal, your song;
The shameful story of your intercourse
With—fiend or woman? And your burning will.
Even in that horror, to the Highest; at last
Your choice of me—the middle course of them,
Pure human love? And, if your song be true,
As I, who heard the voice, the earnestness,
Saw the deep eyes, and truth aflame in them,
Know—then the choice be Mary's and not mine!
I love you better, were that possible;
Will make you a true wife, and lead your hand,
Or be led by you, in the pleasant path.
For me, I enter not—Blesséd be God!—
In those dark problems that disturb your soul.
Mine is the simple nature. Look at me!

### Tannhäuser.

O Lady pure, miracle of true love,
I have a bitter word and harsh to say.
This is my curse—no sooner do I speak,
Or formulate my mind in iron words,
That my mind grows, o'erleaps the limit set,
And I perceive the truth that lies beyond—
One further step into a new-fallen night.
Hear then—I hate to hurt your perfect soul;
I hate myself because I love you still
In that strange intermediate consciousness,

The reason and the mind! This middle way
Ancients called safe—that damns it instantly!
Without some danger nothing great is done!
Let me be God! Or, failing of that task,
Were it but by an unit, let me fall!
And, falling, be it from so great a height
That I may reach some uttermost Abyss,
Inhabit it and reign, most evil one
Of all the Horrors there—and in that path
Seem, even deluded, to approach once more
Infinity. For all the limitless
Hath no distinction—evil is no more,
And good no more.

#### Elizabeth.

But God is absolute Good!

#### Tannhäuser.

No! He is Not! That negative alone
Shadows His shadow to our mortal mind.

#### Elizabeth.

That is too deep; I cannot fathom you.

#### Tannhäuser.

Define, give utterance to this "Good." You see
God slips you, He the Undefinable!
Not good! Not wise! Not anything at all
That heart can grasp, or reason frame, or soul

Shadow the sense of!

**Elizabeth.**

He is far too great!
I see!

**Tannhäuser.**

Not great! The consciousness of man
Their many generations moulded so
To fix in definite ideas, and clothe
Their Maker in the rags. If skies are vast,
So gems are tiny: who shall choose between?
Who reads the riddle of the Universe?
All words! Thus, from his rock-wrought peeking-
point
    Out speers the hermit. "See, the sun is dead!"
It shines elsewhere. You from your tiny perch,
The corner of the corner of the earth,
Itself a speck in solar life; the sun,
For all I know, a speck among the stars,
Themselves one corporate molecule of space!—
You from your perch judge, label, limit Him!
Not that your corner is not equally
The centre and the whole. Fool's talk it is!
Consider the futility of mind!
Realize utterly how mean, how dull,
How fruitless is Philosophy!

**Elizabeth.**

Indeed

My brain is baffled. But I see your point.
Talking of God, even imagining,
Insane! But for aspiring—that I will!

### Tannhäuser.

That is true marriage, in my estimate.
Aspire together to one Deity?
Yes! But to love thee otherwise than that?

### Elizabeth.

This one thing clearly do I understand:
We shall not marry. It is well, my lord.

### Tannhäuser.

Miserable, miserable me! I bring
Hate and disruption and unhappiness
Unto all purity I chance to touch.
I have no hope but I am fallen now;
So journey, in this purpose of despair,
To Lilith and the Venusberg.

### Elizabeth.

Oh no!
Grant me one boon—the one that I shall ask
Ever in this world! Promise me!

### Tannhäuser.

Alas!
One promise gave I once to woman—that
Drove me to this illusion of your love,
And broke your heart.

### Elizabeth.

Oh no, I shall not die.
Have I not Mary and the angels yet?

### Tannhäuser.

You are so pure, so pitiful—your word
Cannot bring evil. Yes, I promise you!

### Elizabeth.

Go then the bitter pilgrimage to Rome,
Gain absolution for this piteous past
From him that owns the twin all-opening keys
That bar your infinite on either side.
Then! look with freshness, hope, and fortitude
Still to the summit—the ideal God.

### Tannhäuser.

I have no hope nor trust in man at all;
But I will go. Fare well, Elizabeth!
       [*Going, returns and kneels before her.*]
Dare you once kiss these grey and withered brows?
As 'twere some flower that fell amid my hair,

The lotus of eternal hope and life.

### Elizabeth.

Dare I? I kiss you once upon the brow,
Praying that God will make the purpose clear,
And on the eyes—that He may lend them light.
        [*Tannhäuser rises, and silently departs.*]
Oh God! Oh God! That I have loved him so!
Be merciful! Be merciful! to him,
The great high soul, bound in the lofty sin;
To me, the little soul, the little sin!

# ACT V.

"One birth of my bosom;
One beam of mine eye;
One topmost blossom
That scales the sky.
Man, equal and one with me, man that is made of me, man that is I."

Hertha.

A desolate and melancholy wood. Nightfall.

### Heinrich.

WELL, I am lost! The whistle brings no hound,
The horn no hunter! North and South are mixed
In this low twilight and the hanging boughs.
I have slept worse than this. Poor Tannhäuser!
I met him walking, as in dream, across
The courtyard, while behind him skulked that crew
That lurked, and itched to kill him, him unarmed,
Not daring! But he reached his hand to me!
"Good luck, old friend!" and, smiling, he was gone.
Gone to the Pope—Great soul to mountebank!
It was her wish, they whisper. Well-a-day!

125

He's gone, and not a friend have I again.
This bank is soft with delicate white moss,
No pillow better in broad Germany.
Were Madeline but here! What rustle stirs
These leaves? A strong man sobbing! The earth quakes
Responsive. Hillo-ho! Who comes by there?

[*Tannhäuser enters. He appears old and worn; but from his whole body radiates a dazzling light, and his face is that of the Christ crucified.*]

Save us, Saints, save us! I have looked on God!

### Tannhäuser.

Heinrich! my friend, my old true-hearted friend!
Fear not! I am not ghost, but living man!
Ah me, ah me, the sorrow of the world!

### Heinrich.

Thou, Tannhäuser! what miracle is this?
Your body glows—with what unearthly light?

### Tannhäuser.

I did not know. Ah! sorrow of this earth!
What tears are falling from the Pleiades!
What sobs tear out Orion's jewelled heart!
Ah me! As these, as these!

### Heinrich.

Speak, speak to me!
Else, I am feared. Why run these tears to earth?
Why shakes your bosom? Why does glory flame
A crown, a cincture? What befell you there?

### Tannhäuser.

I came to Rome across the winter snows
Barefoot, and through the lovely watered land
Rich in the sunshine—even unto Rome.
There knelt I with the other sinful folk
At the great chair of Peter. Sobbed they out
From full repentant hearts their menial sins,
And got them peace. But I told brutally
(Cynical phrase, contempt of self and him)
My sojourn in the Venusberg; then he
Rose in his wrath, and shook the barren staff
Over my head, and cried—I heard his voice
Most like the dweller of the hurricane
Calm, small, and still, directing desolation;
Death to the world athwart its path.—So he
Cried out upon me "Till this barren staff
Take life, and bud, and blossom, and bear fruit,
And shed sweet scent—so long God casteth thee
Out from His glory!" Stricken, smitten, slain—
When—one unknown, a pilgrim with the rest,
Darting long rugged fingers and deep eyes,
Reached to the sceptre with his word and will—
Buds, roses, blossoms! Lilies of the Light!
Bloom, bloom, the fragrance shed upon the air!
Out flames the miracle of life and love!·

Out, out the lights! Flame, flame, the rushing storm!
Darkness and death, and glory in my soul!
Swept, swept away are pope and cardinal,
Palace and city! There I lay beneath
The golden roof of the eternal stars,
Borne up on some irremeable sea
That glowed with most internal brilliance;
Borne up, borne up by hands invisible
Into a firmament of secret light
Manifest, open, permeating me!
Then, then, I cried upon the mystic Word!
(That once begot in me the Venusberg)
And lo! that light was darkness—in the face
Of That which gleamed above. And verily
My life was borne on the dark stream of death
Down whirling aeons, linked abysses, columns
Built of essential time. And lo! the light
Shed from Her shoulders whom I dimly saw;
Crowned with twelve stars and hornéd as the moon;
Clothed with a sun to which the sun of earth
Were tinsel; and the moon was at Her feet—
A moon whose brilliance breaks the sword of song
Into a million fragments; so transcends
Music, that starlight-sandalled majesty!
Then—shall I contemplate the face of Her?
O Nature! Self-begotten! Spouse of God,
The Glory of thy Countenance unveiled!
Thy face, O mother! Splendour of the Gods!
Behold! amid the glory of her hair
And light shed over from the crown thereof,
Wonderful eyes less passionate than Peace
That wept! That wept! O mystery of Love!
Clasping my hands upon the scarlet rose

That flamed upon my bosom, the keen thorns
Pierced me and slew! My spirit was withdrawn
Into Her godhead, and my soul made One
With the Great Sorrow of the Universe,
The Love of Isis! Then I fell away
Into some old mysterious abyss
Rolling between the heights of starry space;
Flaming above, beyond the Tomb of Time,
Blending the darkness into the profound
Chasms of matter—so I fell away
Through many strange eternities of Space,
Limitless fields of Time. I knew in me
That I must fall into the ground and die;
Dwell in the deep a-many years, at last
To rise again—Osiris, slain and risen!
Light of the Cross, I see Thee in the sky,
My future! I must perish from the earth,
Abide in desolate halls, until the hour
When a new Christ must needs be crucified.—
So weep I ever with Our Lady's tears,
Weep for the pain, the travail, the old curse;
Weep, weep, and die. So dawns at last the Grail,
The Glory of the Crucified! Dear friend,
Be happy, for my heart goes out to you,
And most to that poor pale Elizabeth—
Were it not only that the selflessness
That fills me now, forbids the personal,
Casts out the individual, and weeps on
For the united sorrow of all things.
For if I die, it is not Tannhäuser,
Rather a spark of the supreme white light
That dwelt and flickered in him in old time;
That Light, I say, that hides its flame awhile

To shine more fully—to redeem the world!
I say, then, "I"; and yet it is not "I"
Distinct, but "I" incorporate in All.
I am, the Resurrection and the Life!
The Work is finished, and the Night rolled back!
I am the Rising Sun of Life and Light,
The Glory of the Shining of the Dawn!
I am Osiris! I the Lord of Life
Triumphant over death.—

O Sorrow, Sorrow, Sorrow of the World!

### Heinrich.

This was my friend. Deep night descends, perfused
With unsubstantial glory from beyond.
The stars are buried in the mist of light.
Beyond the hill the world is, and laments
Existence—the wide firmament of woe!
And he—his heart was great enough for all,
The fall of sparrows as the crash of stars,
The tears of lonely forests, and the pain
Of the least atom—all were in his heart.
Was that indeed the truth? that he should come
At last a Christ upon the waiting world,
Redeem it to more purpose than the last!
So fills his sorrow, and Her sympathy,
My common soul, that I am fain to fall
Upon my face, and cry aloud to God:
"O Thou, Sole Wise, Sole Pure, Sole Merciful,
Who hast thus shewn Thy mystery to man:
Grant that his coming may be very soon!"
See, the sobs shake me like a little child.

The moon is crescent, waxing in the West.
Take the last kiss, dear.
What is the strange song?
> *The great Goddess ariseth, weeping* for the
slain Osiris Tannhäuser.

### Isis.

Isis am I, and from my life are fed
All stars and suns, all moons that wax and wane,
Create and uncreate, living and dead,
The Mystery of Pain.
I am the Mother, I the silent Sea,
The Earth, its travail, its fertility.
Life, death, love, hatred, light, darkness, return to me

—

To Me!

# PRESS NOTICES

## "GOLDEN OPINIONS
## FROM ALL SORTS OF PEOPLE"

"A windbag foaming at the mouth."

"How rich and melodious are many of his poems, besides being full of powerful and original thought."

"Exquisite stanzas ... many faults."

"Remarkable mastery of form."

"Nearly akin to verbiage ... he has imagination and not infrequently the poet's touch."

"Intense spirituality ... technical superiorities ... an utterance at once mysterious and vivid ... an impressive and original voice ... fiery and clear measured and easy of phrasing."

"Always melodiously ... sometimes nonsensically."

"A sinister rival to the mutoscope."

"Self-revelation of an intensely passionate nature, expressed with a rare command of poetic form ... largely Pagan in sentiment."

"Clever imitations of a brilliant yet somewhat leprous style ... gilded nastiness."

"Veils a morbidly exaggerated Catholicism under an ultra-Egyptian passion for death.... Aleister Crowley is a true poet."

"We quote ... There is a good deal of similar drivel further on."

"Real and striking gifts both of imagination and expression."

"Mr Crowley out-Swinburne's Mr Swinburne.... Shows no mean technical accomplishment."

"The pupil is in some ways greater than the master (Mr Swinburne)."

"Most exalted moods of mysticism ... richness and visionary splendour of the imagery and the aptness and transfiguring power of the rhythms ... plastic and intensely dramatic ... this poet is authentic and will reveal to the world much new beauty...."

"A kind of middle-class Swinburne at secondhand ... morbid unpleasantness of Mr Crowley's taste."

"Much to attract and not a little to repel. A very singular and striking piece of work ... undoubted power and originality ... vigorous mastery and daring conception ... we are compelled to read even where the subject matter fails to attract ... several glaring crudities and much banality."

"An unusual number of gory phantoms."

"A trifle ludicrous and monotonous."

"A riot of words without much thought at the back of them ... windy and boyish in over-emphasis ... very respectable verse."

"Earliest and worst manner of Keats ... no new note here. Even the epithets are conventional...."

"Lacks utterly originality ... echoes of Mr Swinburne, Tennyson, and sometimes of Mr Gilbert."

"Sickly, sensuous vein."

"Holds the first place among the latter-day poets."

"The fairest promise of not only good but great work to come ... has the prophet's vision ... verse worthy of the greatness of his theme ... all the attributes of a true poet."

"Elaborate and perverse ... the most irresistible trait he can find in a maiden is that she should bite like a mad dog ... Mr Crowley is a strong and genuine poet."

# HOUSEHOLD GODS:
# A COMEDY

Graphics and textual content produced by Lolaness.
HOUSEHOLD GODS

A Comedy By Aleister Crowley
[Privately Printed in 1912]

TO LEILA WADDELL

## SCENE

THE HEARTH OF CRASSUS; AFTERWARDS THE LAWNS, THE WOODS, THE LAKE, THE ISLE.

## CHARACTERS

CRASSUS, a barbarian from Britain.

ADELA, his wife, a noble Roman lady.

ALICIA, a servant in the house.

A STATUE OF PAN.

A FAUN.

# HOUSEHOLD GODS

THE SCENE is at the hearth of CRASSUS, where is a little bronze altar dedicated to the Lares and Penates. A pale flame rises from the
burning sandal-wood, on which CRASSUS throws benzoin and musk.
He is standing in deep dejection.

### CRASSUS.

Smoke without fire!
  No thrill of tongues licks up
  The offerings in the cup.
Dead falls desire.

Black smoke thou art,
  O altar-flame, that dost dismember,
  Devour the hearth, to leave no ember
To warm this heart.

I see her still -
  Adela dancing here
  Till dim gods did appear
To work our will.

The delicate girl!
  Diaphanous gossamer
  Subtly revealing her

Brave breast of pearl!

Now - she's withdrawn
  At dusk to the wild woods,
  Mystic beatitudes
That dure till dawn.

Let life exclaim
  Against these things of spirit,
  Mankind that disinherit
Of love's pure flame!
[He bends before the altar and begins to weep.]

Ye household gods!
  By these male tears I swear
  That ye shall grant this prayer.
All things at odds
Shall be put straight -
  Harmonized, reconciled
  By some appointed child
Of some far Fate!
[A curtain has been drawn aside during this invoca-
tion, and

    ALICIA advances. She smiles subtly upon him; and,
giving a strange gesture, makes one or two noiseless steps
of dancing.]


**ALICIA.**


Master still sad?

## CRASSUS.

These faint and fearful shores
  Of time are beaten by the surge of sense,
  Love worn away - by love? - to indifference.
Who knows what god - or demon - she adores?
  Or in what wood she shelters, or what grove
  Sees her profane our sacrament of love?

### ALICIA.

I saw her follow
The stream in the hollow
Where never Apollo
  Abides.
So thick are the trees
That never the breeze
Stirs them, or sees
  What satyr inhabits the glen, what nymph in the
    pools of it hides.

Lighter of foot
  Than a sylph or a fairy,
  Sinuous, wary,
  I passed from the airy
Lawns, where the flute
  Of the winds made tremulous music for man.

I followed the ripple
  Of the stream; I crept
  Where the waters wept -
    The floss in the foss
    Gurgling across
    The bosses of moss,
Like a dryad's nipple

145

In the mouth of Pan!

### CRASSUS.

O pearl of the house! you came to the end?

### ALICIA.

The dusk of the slave, the dawn of a friend?

### CRASSUS.

Freedom is thine for the skill and the will.

### ALICIA.

The skill is mine - but the will lies still,
Still as the earth that dare not stir
Till the kiss of the sun awaken her!

### CRASSUS.

Yet at these secrets and riddles? Behold!
I can fill thy lap with a harvest of gold.

### ALICIA.

Yet all the gold you could give to me
Would fall at my feet when I rose to be free.

## CRASSUS.

What will you then?

## ALICIA.

No gift from men.
Of my own free will I give you wit,
(O man so sorely in need of it!)
And happiness; and the flame that hath dwindled
On this dull hearth shall be rekindled.
But this you must swear:
To will, and to dare,
To seek the spirit and slay the sense;
  And for this hour
  To give me power
To lead you in silent obedience,
Though I bade you fall on your sword....

## CRASSUS.

Enough!
I give my life as I gave my love.

## ALICIA.

O! love you have not understood.
You have not guessed its secret food.
You have not seen its single eye;
But fear and doubt and jealousy
Have risen, and now your love is trembling
Like a mountebank dissembling
When his trick's detected. Come!

To find home we must leave home.

### CRASSUS.

Starless and moonless, hidden in cloud,
The night's one flame of pearl.

### ALICIA.

The bat flaps; the owl hoots aloud.

### CRASSUS.

Lead on; I trust you, girl.

### ALICIA.

You are bold to trust me; or, have you divined
My secret?

### CRASSUS.

No; the crystal of your mind
Shows only faint disturbing images,
Things passing strange, as if enchanted seas
Kept their great swell upon it, and strange fish
Played in its oily depths. Some monstrous wish,
The shadow of some unspeakable desire,
Strikes my heart cold, and sets my brain on fire.

ALICIA.

Learn this, as we pass through the portico:
Fear nothing; there is nothing you can know!
And by these terraces and steps that gleam
Wintry, although the summer night is hot,
This - what we seek is never what we find!

Life is a dream, like love; and from the dream
If we may wake, we never find it what
We would; for the wisdom of a mightier mind
Leads us in its own ways
To a perfected praise.

CRASSUS.

Why are these shadows thrown across the lawn
From the elms and yews? They were not wont to
reach
Beyond the branches of that copper-beech.

ALICIA.

Attend the dawn
Of an unknown comet, that shall come
From the unfathomable wells of space
Into its halidom.

CRASSUS.

I know it not. Last night I walked alone
Here, and saw nothing.

## ALICIA.

I was not with you!
There is no God upon the eternal throne
Of stars begemming the bewildering blue
Unless one has the eyes to see him. Think
How we two stand upon the brink
Of nothing! Here's a globe, whereto we trust,
No larger than the smallest speck of dust
Or mote in the sunbeam is to that sun's self,
And we are like dead leaves in autumn's whil
Of wind upon it.

## CRASSUS.

Mystify me, girl!
It is the right of an elf.
Surely your flickering fire
Will draw me to some mire!

## ALICIA.

Here the stream dips its mouth into the wood.
So does youth's calm and chaste beatitude
Touch the black mouth of Love, the ancient whore.

## CRASSUS.

Girl! what a scorpion leaping from your lips!

## ALICIA.

My mouth stings as no scorpion ever stang.

in this round impudent smiling face of mine
There is a poison fiercer than all wine;
And from these eyes more subtle sorrows pour
Than you can dream. These teeth have been at grips
With gods; I have sung what no girl ever sang.
These ears have heard
An insufferable word!

CRASSUS.

What do you mean?

ALICIA.

The secret's in a kiss.
Here are no kisses. Here great Artemis
Rules; only in the woodland may a man
Hide his eyes from her, pledge himself to Pan.
Come! through the tangled arches
Of cypresses and larches,
Stoop; under Artemis we walked upright;
But this is Pan's home, and the House of Night.
[They enter the wood.]

CRASSUS.

So when I stoop, my cheek comes close to yours.
Give me a kiss.

ALICIA.

The poisonous apple lures
Thus the boy's mouth. Beware!

**CRASSUS.**

O you are fair!
Fairer than ever! In this tangle of trees
Your hot breath wraps you in perfume.

**ALICIA.**

There is some gloom or doom,
A bitter harsh ingredient
In these my sorceries
Of animal scent.

**CRASSUS.**

Yes! there is fear mixed with the fascination.
It is the reverence that chastity, be sure!
Gains from the impure.

**ALICIA.**

O virtuous nation!
It is the fear of the uninitiate
Before the throne of Fate
The hierophant.

**CRASSUS.**

Kiss me, however!

ALICIA.

Did I grant
This favour, all were lost. It is your truth
To Adela that tempts my youth.
  [Henceforth Alicia shakes with silent laughter.]

CRASSUS.

What little breasts you have!

ALICIA.

Ay, maiden breasts!
Would you betray my oath?

CRASSUS.

My will contests
My wishes.

ALICIA.

Wait, and you shall surely see
Part of the secret that ensorcels me.
See all these bosses! It is not
As if a Titan smote himself into the earth,
And was caught into her, made one with her?

CRASSUS.

The scent is fierce and hot
Like a rutting panther's slot.

153

Yet you are matched with mirth,
Shaking each other like two wrestlers.

### ALICIA.

What should stir
Your melancholy but laughter?

### CRASSUS.

Look, before us
Light streams, a tremulous chorus.
Oh, it is vague and vacillating!

### ALICIA.

Love,
Young love of maidens, is the soul thereof.
And in the midst, behold, O man!
The image of great Pan.

### CRASSUS.

I fear him.

### ALICIA.

Go and lie there, at his feet.
Lie supine! Lie on that moss-covered root,
While I draw forth the flute
And make a marvellous music.

       [She ceases laughing and begins to play.]

## CRASSUS.

O I writhe
Beneath the force of lips, of fingers lithe
That touch the delicate stops so delicately.

## ALICIA.

Hush!
I have drawn the bird from the bush.
Pan will appear anon.

## CRASSUS.

Ah! Ah! ... Ah! Ah!

## ALICIA.

This music moves you. Now I'll play a tune
That would make mad the melancholy moon.
This.

## CRASSUS.

Ah! you tear my soul out with the trills.

Your fingers play like summer lightning on the shaft.

It is like a storm on the mountains when it shrills;
Like the angry sea when it booms. Hark!

## ALICIA.

Some god laughed.

### CRASSUS.

Your mouth is like some god's It burns and blooms
With fire unheard of, with unguessed perfumes.
O let me kiss you!

### ALICIA.

So you stop my song!
                    [She ceases the tune.]

### CRASSUS.

There is another song.

### ALICIA.

You do me wrong.
For you love Adela!

### CRASSUS.

By God, girl, no!
I love Alicia.

### ALICIA.

Ah! you love her SO! [She laughs]

### CRASSUS.

Your laugh is shocking - why do you mock me, dear?

ALICIA.

Because you will not guess my secret here.
But - put your arms about my neck, and swar
You love me, and will always keep them there.
Then I might dare.

CRASSUS.

I swear it. O my sweet!

ALICIA.

Then take my kiss.

CRASSUS.

Your mouth is like a rose of fire. But what is this?
I cannot bear it.

ALICIA.

Ai! Uhu! Uhu!
It is my heart; this arrow strikes me through.
Stir not one muscle for a moment. Death!
You beast, you kill me with your urgent breath.

CRASSUS.

O how I love you! [He moves violently.]

### ALICIA.

Fool! Now all my pain
Must be gone through again.
It is sure your chastity's unstained by crime;
You do the wrong thing just at the right time!

### CRASSUS.

Why do you taunt me? All the wood is spring's,
And love is hovering o'er us with his wings.

### ALICIA.

Sub pennis, penis!

### CRASSUS.

Hush! you break the spell.

### ALICIA.

Oh! you great fools fo men, I know you well.
But nothing is so detrimental
To love as to be sentimental.
I will yet make you wise.
Know that I have the magic to disguise
Myself in many ways. Do you feel this?
(Lie still, this heaven were ruined by a kiss!)
I am a butterfly, such idle flitting
As to a flower like you is fitting
Now I'm a mole. Do you think you know me now?
Here is the earthworm severed by the plough.

CRASSUS.

You are a witch. I want your love; you give
Only love's comedy.

ALICIA.

The way to live
Is to find comedy and tragedy
In everything. But if you cannot see
Through to the Bacchanal spirit, this should suit.
Here is the blacksmith hammering a flute.

CRASSUS.

Oh love, love, kiss me!

ALICIA.

I will forge a ring
Of bloom of blood-kisses upon your neck,
Till it is like a garden of roses in late spring.

CRASSUS.

"Soft, and stung softly, fairer for a fleck."

ALICIA.

O marvellous nation!
Vanity, dullness, slobber, and quotation!

## CRASSUS.

Why do you love me if you scorn me so?

## ALICIA.

Why, did I say I loved you? I say no.

## CRASSUS.

Why do you make love?

## ALICIA.

To beguile the hour;
To crown my rose-wreath with a greener flower'
To do my master's bidding, that's to give
Life to yourself, who only think you live.
But listen! Have you seen the nine waves roll
Monotonous upon the shoal,
Rising and falling like a maiden asleep;
Then with a lift and a leap
The ninth wave curls, and breaks upon the beach,
And rushes up it, swallowing the sand?
I am that ocean.... Now, you understand?

## CRASSUS.

Alicia! O! this is unbearable.
Surely this wave washes the shore of hell!

**ALICIA.**

Each follows each
Remorseless and indifferent as Nature
Is to each creature.

**CRASSUS.**

Wonderful, wonderful woman!

[She throws her head back, and laughs]

**ALICIA.**

Now, you think
You know my secret. I have given you drink,
And you are wise. But hush! to all emotion
Save this the pulse and swell of Ocean
For at the last with mouth and fingers wried
All must proclaim the triumph of the tide.

**CRASSUS.**

Ah! still you mock me with your cruel laugh.

**ALICIA.**

It is your foolish epitaph.

**CRASSUS.**

But this can be no mockery. Heave and sway
And curl and thrust - these waves are not at play.

161

## ALICIA.

You feel the ocean breaking on the shoal;
But passionless and moveless is its soul.

## CRASSUS.

Ah! but your soul is in your breath.

## ALICIA.

Only as the graven image of death
Which men call life, and ignorantly adore!

## CRASSUS.

Spare me! I cannot bear you more.

## ALICIA.

Then will I drown you. Lock your fingers fast
In mind, and let our mouths mix at the last.

[The statue of PAN is seen to be alive.]

## PAN.

Shrill, shrill
Over the hill!
The hunter is hot - this is the kill!
Scream! Scream!
Dissolving the dream

Of life, the knife to the heart of the wife!
The fountain jets
Its flood of blood,
And the moss that it wets
Is an amethyst flame of violets.

Who shall escape
Murder and rape
What I am alive in my solemn shape?
Shrill, shrill,
Over the hill!
The hunter is hot - this is the kill!
The heart of the home
Is a fury of foam;
The storm is awake, and the billows comb.
But though I be
Their frenzy of glee,
I am also the passionless soul of the sea!

Mine eyes glint fire,
And my cruel lips curl;
Mine the desire
Of the god and the girl;
But fierier and fleeter,
And subtler and sweeter
Than the race of the rhythm, the march of the me-
tre,
Is the shrilling, shrilling
Of the knife in the killing
That ends, when it must,
(O the throb and the thrust!)
In a death, in the dust,
The silence, the stillness, of satiate lust,

163

The solemn pause
When the veil withdraws
And man looks on his god, on the Causeless Cause.
Still, still,
Under the hill!
The hunter is dead - this is the kill!

### CRASSUS.

Pan spoke.

### ALICIA.

Pan never speaks till man is dumb,
And only then if he be like a child
Silently curled within its mother's womb,
Or feeding at her breast. There is a wild
Way also - when his dumbness is of death.
And there's a first and second death. Remember
To die so that no god's or angel's breath
May quicken into life the wasted ember!

### CRASSUS.

I am dead now.

### ALICIA.

But I must raise you up.
The night grows darker; all Pan's light is gone,
And you and I are pledged to sup
Upon a secret.

CRASSUS.

All your secret shone.
[She laughs again.]

ALICIA.

Oh, when you know it! But you must divine
Adela's shrine.

CRASSUS.

I am weary of Adela grown chaste and chill.

ALICIA.

The hunter lags; how heavy is the hill!
But you are bound to Adela.

CRASSUS.

To you!

ALICIA.

But you have given me freedom. I will leave you.

CRASSUS.

What have I done to grieve you?

165

## ALICIA.

You have been the solemn fool with face awry
That I have gathered in my ecstasy.
You are only a vulgar primrose I have plucked.

## CRASSUS.

At least, she-devil, you have been well-treated.

## ALICIA.

O tragic farce - not even rimes completed!
Nay, darling! no rebellion. When you know
My secret, you will understand. You are bound
To Adela within the portico,
To me upon this ground.
By day, in life, adore the Lares, man!
By night, in death, make offering to Pan!
Can you cut day from night by any endeavour?
If so, both life and death were lost for ever.
Come, the stream steepens.

## CRASSUS.

This road leads to hell.

## ALICIA.

The way to heaven is shorter.

CRASSUS.

Who can tell?

ALICIA.

I have measured it.

CRASSUS.

You, girl?

ALICIA.

It is not hard.

CRASSUS.

What did you make the height of it?

ALICIA.

One yard.

CRASSUS.

You always mock me?

ALICIA.

Pity of my youth!
I swerve not from, you stumble at, the truth.

## CRASSUS.

I like not jests. This is a serious journey.

## ALICIA.

Why did you make a mocker your attorney?
The way to Rome leads through the Apennines.
Bacchus has horns beneath the crown of vines.
If you fear horns, make some polite excuse
Not to invoke him by the name Zagreus!

## A FAUN [Passing among the trees].

Ye thought me a lamb
 With a crown of thorns;
am royal, a ram
With death in my horns.
So mild and soft
 And feminine,
Ye held me aloft
 And frowned on sin!
But I was awake
 In your clasp as I lay;
I roused the snake
 From its nest of clay;
And ere ye knew
I had sunk my forehead
Through and through;
 Harsh and horrid
Through all the pleasure
 Of rose and vineI thrust my treasure,

The cone of the pine.
Irru's maid
Was easily sated,
For she was afraid
When Irru mated!

CRASSUS.

Ha! Ha! Ha! Ha! Ha! Ha!

ALICIA.

You would not laugh
Were you the maid!

CRASSUS.

How could I be?

ALICIA.

Great calf!
But you are all the same, blaspheme and jeer
At any mystery beyond your sphere
Of beer, and beef, and beer, and beef, and beer.
Now you have frightened the shy god!

CRASSUS.

Why heed?
Between your - arms - is all the god I need.

**ALICIA.**

Prudish and coarse to the last. Now hush indeed!
The stream kisses the lake. We near the shrine.
Stir no snapped twig. Let your foot - even yours -
Fall like a fawn's.

**CRASSUS.**

Your breath is like new wine.

**ALICIA.**

Hush now! no porpoise gambols!

**CRASSUS.**

How obscure's
The glimmer of the lake. Is that the isle?

**ALICIA.**

Yes! in that shadow lurks a smile.
See; from that jagged cloud Diana starts
Like a deer from the brake; her silver splendour
darts
Through the crisp air to the grove upon the isle...
Do you see her? Do you see her?

**CRASSUS.**

Monstrous! Vile!

These eyes betray me.

**ALICIA.**

No! your Adela lies
With arms thrown back, head tilted, open thighs.
Her lips flame out like poppies in the dusk.
The breeze brings back to us a scent of musk.
Her mouth is oozing kisses!

**CRASSUS.**

Filthy harlot!

**ALICIA.**

I never fed on a superber scarlet.
And look! the wonder of plumes that foams upon
Her tidal breast - oh, but a swan! a swan!
A swan snow-white with his sole scarlet hidden
In the abode forbidden!

O but his eye swoons as his broad beak slips
Within her luscious lips.
O but - I cannot see - I long to die
Alike for wonder - and for jealousy!

**CRASSUS.**

Vile, filthy whore! I'll catch you at it.

#### ALICIA.

Soft!
See how his feathers hold her soul aloft!

#### CRASSUS.

Beast! Have you brought me through the wood for this?

#### ALICIA.

Now wonder I must teach you how to kiss.

#### CRASSUS.

I'll clip his wings.

#### ALICIA.

Sub pennis, penis! 'Slife!
It's not the wings of him that clip your wife.

#### CRASSUS.

Thou art as filthy a creature as she!

#### ALICIA.

Fat fool!
All your emotions vary with your -

CRASSUS.

What?

ALICIA.

Your state of health.

CRASSUS.

Be off with you, foul —

ALICIA.

Well?

CRASSUS.

I'll swim and stab them. The black mouth of hell
Yawns for their murder.

ALICIA.

I'll be at the death.
Dive then, but softly. Scarcely draw your breath.

CRASSUS.

O, she's unwary!

### ALICIA.

Is your love forgotten?

### CRASSUS.

All love is rotten.

### ALICIA.

But your pure love for me you boasted of?

### CRASSUS.

Ay, that was perfect love.

### ALICIA.

You love me then, not her?

### CRASSUS.

Indeed I do.

### ALICIA.

Swear me the oath anew!

### CRASSUS.

I swear to love you till the world shall end.

ALICIA.

Then, Crassus, I will always be your friend.

CRASSUS.

Ah, that is good! You do not mock me now!

ALICIA.

Creep softly to the land. Kiss but my brow.
My curls are wet... No, never touch me there!

CRASSUS.

Why? Have I not?

ALICIA.

You have not.

CRASSUS.

Just my hand.

ALICIA.

You disobey your mistress's command?
The time is near when you shall see
The keyhole of my comedy!

### CRASSUS.

Ha! Ha! Ha!

### ALICIA.

Hush, you coarse slave; we'll surprise
Your good wife in her mystic exercise.
Quick, through the bramble!
                    [They burst through upon ADELA.]

### CRASSUS.

Now, you beast, I've got you!
The curst of God, and plague of Naples, rot you!
For this white brute - one slit!
                    [He cuts the throat of THE SWAN
with his dagger.]

### ADELA.

Oh love betrayed!
O my dead beauty! Faugh! deceitful maid.
Not Crassus found me out. Had I the wings
Of my dead love - oh love! -

### ALICIA.

Why, wondrous things!

**ADELA.**

These nails shall serve. A servant!

**CRASSUS.**

She shall be
My wife, damned witch, when I have done with
thee!
[THE SWAN dies.]

**ADELA.**

I'll kill her now. But see! my swan is dead.

**ALICIA.**

Yes! and what light is breaking overhead?
What blaze of blue and gold envelops us?

**CRASSUS.**

O marvel! O miraculous!

**ADELA.**

What is it? Why, my lover's life, in me
Once concentrated, now diffused, illumes
The endless reaches of eternity
With infinite brilliance, with intense perfumes.

## ALICIA.

O then your lover was some god's disguise.

## ADELA.

And you have robbed me. Now beware your eyes!
        [She springs at ALICIA, who guards herself
        easily. But in the struggle her robe tears.]

## ALICIA.

Take care!

## ADELA.

A boy!

## CRASSUS.

A boy! Then what am I?

## ALICIA.

That is the key-word of the comedy.
You thought you had two vices at your need;
But she had Jove and you had Ganymede.
        [They are struck dumb and still with
        amazement. ALICIA claps her hands
        four times.]

Sweep through the air, bright blaze of eagle-wings!
Crassus, sub pennis, penis! How he swings

His bulk from yonder sightless poise, to bear
me back to the Dominion of the air
Where I shall bear the cup of Jupiter!
Blind babes, love one another, no less true
Because the gods have deigned to dwell with you!
[The eagle bears GANYMEDE aloft.]


CRASSUS.

Adela! these mysteries too great
For you and me to estimate.
But, widowed both, come, seek domestic charms
As we were wont, in one another's arms!
What perfect moss for you to lie upon!
ADELA. I am your wife, dear Crassus.
(sotto voce) Oh, my swan!

CURTAIN.

# Reader's Guide

# Table of Contents

# INTRODUCTION TO THE
# READER'S GUIDE

Aleister Crowley is too often remembered for the myth instead of the mind behind it. The sensational figure preserved in tabloids and rumor obscures a disciplined thinker, dramatist, and philosopher whose work engages deeply with questions of purpose, freedom, and interior transformation. To read him attentively is to encounter not an eccentric curiosity, but a writer who used art to examine the human condition with unusual clarity and daring.

The plays that precede this guide sit at the intersection of literature, ritual, and psychological inquiry. They are not merely scripts to be staged, but meditations in dramatic form—works that explore how individuals confront temptation, limitation, and the search for authentic will. Their settings differ, but their aims converge: to show how spiritual and ethical struggle unfolds through lived experience, whether in the register of myth or in the subtler terrain of daily life.

This guide exists to accompany that encounter. It offers context without prescribing interpretation, and illumination without closure. Crowley wrote for readers willing to look beneath the surface, to listen for the symbolic architecture beneath narrative gesture. The commentary and materials collected here are designed to support that effort: not to explain the plays away, but to help the attentive reader see more of what is already present within them.

Crowley's drama is participatory by design. These works assume that the reader brings not only curiosity, but a willingness to reflect. They do not aim to convert, persuade, or instruct by decree; instead, they invite engagement—ethical, psychological, and imaginative. Like the rituals that informed them, they stage a process of awakening rather than a set of conclusions.

Approached in this spirit, the plays reveal why they remain compelling long after their initial composition. Their questions—about will, consequence, responsibility, and inner alignment—belong not to a single era, but to the ongoing drama of human consciousness. They remind us that transformation is not abstract, but lived; not distant, but immediate; not merely mythic, but personal.

This guide is offered in that same spirit: as a companion for the reader already in motion, a framework through which to deepen encounter rather than replace it. The plays stand on their own. What follows is simply a clearer window through which to view them.

# TIMELINE OF CROWLEY'S LIFE

- **1875** – Born *Edward Alexander Crowley* on October 12 in Royal Leamington Spa, England, eldest of three children to Edward Crowley, a brewer, and Emily Bertha Bishop Crowley, a devout Plymouth Brethren Christian.

- **1880s** – Raised in a strict religious environment; begins showing intellectual and artistic talent.

- **1890s** – Attends Malvern College; develops literary skill, interest in philosophy, science, and exploration.

- **1895** – Matriculates at Trinity College, Cambridge, studying mathematics, classics, and literature; finds academic life restrictive.

- **1897–1898** – Undertakes extensive travel in Mexico and North Africa; begins climbing mountains and exploring wilderness.

- **1898** – Joins the *Hermetic Order of the Golden Dawn*; studies ritual magic and mysticism; begins using the name "Aleister" in magical and literary contexts as part of self-fashioning.

- **1900** – Travels through India and China; studies meditation, yoga, and Eastern religions; begins integrating these influences into his philosophical and magical framework.

- **1903** – Marries *Rose Edith Kelly* in Scotland.

- **1904** – During their honeymoon in Cairo, Rose experiences trances that lead Crowley to receive *Liber AL vel Legis* (*The Book of the Law*), establishing the foundation of Thelema.

- **1904–1906** – Birth of their daughter *Lilith*, who dies of typhoid fever in Rangoon; Rose's health declines, and the marriage deteriorates soon after.

- **1907** – Founds the A∴A∴ (Argentum Astrum, or "Silver Star") to provide a structured system for personal and spiritual development through magick, meditation, and study; publishes *Tannhäuser*, demonstrating his dramatic and symbolic literary sensibilities.

- **1908–1912** – Engages in mountaineering across Africa, the Alps, and the Himalayas; completes several first ascents, gaining recognition in climbing circles.

- **1910** – Expelled from the *Hermetic Order of the Golden Dawn* following disputes with leaders, particularly S.L. MacGregor Mathers, over authority and ritual practice.

- **1912–1914** – Publishes *Magick in Theory and Practice* and other key works on ceremonial magick; reforms the *Ordo Templi Orientis* (*O.T.O.*), codifying rituals to reflect Thelemic philosophy.

- **1914–1918** – Travels extensively during World War I; continues literary and ritual work; notoriety grows due to unconventional lifestyle and public perception of his magickal activities.

- **1920** – Establishes the *Abbey of Thelema* in Cefalù, Sicily, with Leah

Hirsig; birth of his daughter *Anne Leah ("Poupée")* with Hirsig.

- **Early 1920s** – Birth of his daughter *Astarte Lulu Panthea* with Ninette Shumway during the Abbey period. These and his earlier daughter *Lilith* with Rose Kelly were his three known children.

- **1923** – Expelled from Italy following controversy surrounding the Abbey of Thelema.

- **1929** – Marries *Maria Teresa Ferrari de Miramar*, a Nicaraguan woman; marriage ends within a year.

- **1930s** – Focuses on literary output, occult instruction, and mentoring; publishes essays, journals, and commentaries exploring philosophy, psychology, and the arts.

- **1940s** – Health declines due to chronic bronchitis and arterial disease; continues writing and guiding students.

- **1947** – Dies on December 1 in Hastings, England; largely unnoticed by the public but revered within occult and literary circles. Buried in the cemetery of the Church of St. Mary and St. Peter in Hastings.

# ALEISTER CROWLEY: A BIOGRAPHY

Aleister Crowley was born Edward Alexander Crowley on October 12, 1875, in Royal Leamington Spa, England. He was the eldest child of Edward Crowley, a wealthy brewer, and Emily Bertha Bishop Crowley, a devout Plymouth Brethren Christian. He had two younger sisters. His upbringing was marked by strict religious discipline, a rigidity he would later rebel against, shaping much of his philosophy and his lifelong antagonism toward conventional morality. Crowley described his early experiences as suffocating, and this tension between imposed belief and personal exploration would become central to his life and work.

From a young age, Crowley displayed exceptional intellectual and artistic talent. He was educated privately and later at Malvern College, where he showed literary skill alongside a fascination with science, philosophy, and exploration. At Trinity College, Cambridge, he pursued mathematics, classics, and literature, though he found academic life constraining. Increasingly drawn to poetry, ritual, and mysticism, he began to explore how consciousness, art, and spiritual practice could be interwoven into a unified philosophical and aesthetic vision.

Crowley's adolescence and early adulthood were defined by travel and adventure. He climbed mountains in Mexico and North Africa, achieving several first ascents that earned him recognition in mountaineering circles. He trekked through India, China, and the Middle East, immersing himself in local religions, meditation, and yoga. These experiences profoundly influenced his later writings and ritual practices, providing a foundation for his integration of Eastern and Western mystical traditions.

In 1898, Crowley began formal study of Western esoteric traditions, joining the Hermetic Order of the Golden Dawn. His time in the Golden Dawn was marked by both achievement and conflict. He clashed repeatedly with senior members, particularly Samuel Liddell MacGregor Mathers, over issues of authority, ritual practice, and the use of secret knowledge. Accusations that he broke order rules and pursued personal agendas ultimately led to his expulsion. Far from discouraging him, this rupture catalyzed the development of his own magickal system, Thelema, based on the principle: "Do what thou wilt shall be the whole of the Law." The experience shaped Crowley's independent approach to ritual, spiritual philosophy, and personal discipline, laying the groundwork for his later founding of the A∴A∴ and reform of the O.T.O.

In 1903, Crowley married Rose Edith Kelly, a union that would unexpectedly alter the course of his spiritual life. During their honeymoon in Cairo, Rose experienced a series of trances in which she declared that the god Horus awaited Crowley's attention. Acting on her words, he performed invocations that culminated in the dictation of *Liber AL vel Legis* (*The Book of the Law*) in April 1904, establishing the central tenets of Thelema: "Do what thou wilt shall be the whole of the Law." The marriage produced one daughter, Lilith, who died of typhoid in 1906, and soon afterward Rose's health and sanity deteriorated, leading to their separation. Decades later, in 1929, Crowley briefly married Maria Teresa Ferrari de Miramar, a Nicaraguan woman whose struggles with mental illness and poverty mirrored his own declining fortunes. Crowley fathered several children over the course of his life. His first daughter, Lilith, with Rose Kelly, died in infancy. Later, during his time at the Abbey of Thelema in Sicily, he had two daughters: Anne Leah ("Poupée") with Leah Hirsig, and Astarte Lulu Panthea with Ninette Shumway.

Crowley was an exceptionally prolific and versatile writer. His literary output included poetry, plays, novels, philosophical treatises, essays, and instructional manuals on ceremonial magick. Notable works include *The Book of the Law* (1904), *Magick in Theory and Practice*, and numerous journals, travelogues, and literary explorations. His plays, such as *Tannhäuser* and *Household Gods*, reveal his dramatic sensibility, philosophical depth, and willingness to confront taboo subjects, while his essays and criticism reflect his engagement with literature, culture, and psychology. Crowley also experimented with translation, commentary, and literary criticism, showing an ambitious intellectual range that extended far beyond occult instruction.

Crowley founded and reformed several organizations to advance his spiritual and philosophical vision. He established the A∴A∴ (Argentum Astrum, or "Silver Star"), an order devoted to disciplined development through magick, meditation, and philosophical study, offering members a structured path to higher consciousness and realization of Thelemic principles. He reformed the Ordo Templi Orientis (O.T.O.), codifying rituals and practices in accordance with Thelema and creating a system often misunderstood or sensationalized by the public. These organizational efforts reflected his commitment to disciplined self-development and intellectual rigor, despite his reputation as a scandalous and provocative figure.

Crowley's life was one of extremes, combining rigorous intellectual and artistic work with a public persona that cultivated controversy. He engaged in rivalries and collaborations with other occultists, literary figures, and social critics. At the same time, he maintained deep friendships with followers and students inspired by his teachings. Beyond esotericism, he was a serious mountaineer, traveler, poet, and thinker, exploring the intersections of psychology, spirituality, and the arts. His journals and travelogues demonstrate a keen observational skill, philosophical reflection, and artistic sensibility.

Crowley died on December 1, 1947, in Hastings, England, from chronic bronchitis aggravated by arterial disease. His death passed largely without public celebration, though within occult and literary circles he was remembered and revered. He is buried in the cemetery of the Church of St. Mary and St. Peter in Hastings, in a simple grave that reflects the paradox of a man who cultivated myth, spectacle, and notoriety, yet ultimately returned to quiet obscurity.

Aleister Crowley remains a complex, multi-faceted figure: a man of letters, philosophy, and ritual; a traveler and explorer; a controversial public persona; and an innovator whose influence resonates in literature, spirituality, and esoteric study. His plays, writings, travels, mountaineering achievements, and organizational work illustrate a life devoted to exploring human consciousness, artistic expression, and spiritual development — a life of extremes, intellect, and creativity that continues to provoke, challenge, and inspire.

# CROWLEY AND THE "WICKEDEST MAN" MYTH

Aleister Crowley's reputation as "the wickedest man in the world" has persisted for more than a century, fueled by sensationalist reporting, rumor, and his own provocative public persona. Yet this label obscures the intellectual, spiritual, and ethical dimensions of his life. Crowley openly defied social norms, particularly in matters of sexuality, engaging in consensual acts—including homosexual relationships—and often incorporating ritualized elements into his practices. He made no apologies for living according to his own principles, and this unapologetic authenticity frequently drew scandalized attention.

The "wickedest man" image exaggerates and misrepresents Crowley's intentions. His acts, while shocking to Victorian and early twentieth-century audiences, were never malicious; they were expressions of personal will and spiritual discipline. Crowley drew extensively from traditions such as Kabbalah and Christian mysticism, both rooted in Right-Hand Path philosophies emphasizing ethical action, self-mastery, and spiritual ascent. Nothing in his practice was truly Left-Hand Path; the purpose of his rituals and unconventional behaviors was alignment with higher consciousness, not harm or transgression for its own sake. As Dr. Stephen E. Flowers notes in *Lords of the Left-Hand Path*, Crowley's work exemplifies disciplined Right-Hand Path approaches, despite outward appearances of transgression.

While he did not attempt to correct misconceptions or tone down his reputation, Crowley often leaned into the myth, understanding that society's reaction could magnify attention to his ideas. His public persona functioned as both performance and pedagogy: it drew curiosity, challenged conventional morality, and created a space in which his philosophy and plays could reach a wider audience. The "wicked" image coexisted with —and even highlighted—the rigor, discipline, and ethical framework underpinning his work.

Crowley's life extended far beyond the scandal that defined his public image. He was a polymath, world traveler, and adventurer. In 1900, he traveled to Mexico, where he immersed himself in ceremonial magick and engaged in a romantic relationship with a local woman. He attempted the first ascent of K2—the second-highest mountain in the world, located on the border between Pakistan and China in the Karakoram Range—in 1902, and later led an expedition on Kanchenjunga. Both endeavors were physically grueling and groundbreaking for their time, reflecting his endurance, courage, and willingness to confront extreme challenges. He also traveled to India, where he studied Rāja yoga and attained states of dhyāna, and spent time in Paris, mingling with artists and intellectuals. These experiences reveal a man of wide-ranging interests, curiosity, and discipline, showing that his intellect and energy were as much directed toward exploration, philosophy, and self-mastery as toward occultism.

By examining Crowley's life alongside his writings, plays, and spiritual practice, it becomes clear that the myth of the "wickedest man" obscures more than it reveals. He was neither immoral nor malevolent; he was unapologetically himself, navigating the world with imagination, discipline, and ethical purpose. The persistence of the myth in contemporary culture demonstrates the enduring power of his persona. In a sense, this enduring legend functions as a form of Crowley's final magickal working: a lasting influence on public consciousness, ensuring that his life, work, and defiance of societal norms continue to fascinate and provoke thought.

# THELEMA AND THE A∴A∴: SPIRITUAL DISCIPLINE ON STAGE

At the heart of Crowley's thought lies Thelema, built on the principle, "Do what thou wilt shall be the whole of the Law." It calls each person to discover their true purpose and live in alignment with it. Crowley saw this as a serious path that required courage, honesty, and attention to the demands of daily life. Life itself became a field of spiritual practice, where each choice and action reflected the deeper currents of will and meaning.

The A∴A∴, or Argentum Astrum, put this vision into practice. It offered a structured program of study, ritual, and reflection designed to harmonize daily life with higher consciousness. Transformation began with mastery of the self and careful awareness of one's surroundings. For Crowley, the work of the A∴A∴ was not abstract. It was lived experience, a demanding journey toward clarity, freedom, and spiritual growth.

In *Tannhäuser*, these principles shape the drama in profound ways. Characters confront temptation and struggle with spiritual aspiration. Their trials and choices dramatize the Thelemic journey, making it immediate and tangible for the audience. The play shows the challenge of acting in accordance with one's deeper purpose and the rewards that come from persistence and insight.

*Household Gods* carries the same current in a domestic, satirical form. Characters contend with routine, social pressures, and the pull of ordinary life while striving to fulfill their deeper aspirations. Crowley's philosophy shapes their arcs subtly, showing that transformation is not limited to mystical experience but emerges from the everyday effort to live with integrity and purpose.

By weaving Thelema and the A∴A∴ into his plays, Crowley turns philosophy into living drama. The stage becomes a place where human desire, intention, and striving are made visible. Audiences witness the challenge of discovering one's will, mastering oneself, and moving toward transformation, both in the drama on stage and in reflection on their own lives.

## Kabbalah — Mapping the Mystical

Kabbalah, the Jewish mystical tradition, profoundly shaped Crowley's imagination. At its center lies the Tree of Life, a symbolic map of creation and of the soul's ascent, traced through ten spheres of being. This image is more than an abstract diagram. It is a vision of how human striving, moral conflict, and divine presence interlock. For Crowley, it offered a living architecture on which drama itself could be built.

In *Tannhäuser*, the architecture underpins the action. The story unfolds like a climb along the Tree of Life: each figure represents a stage of the inner journey, confronting trials, succumbing to or resisting temptation, and glimpsing flashes of revelation. The interplay between passion and discipline, between earthly desire and transcendent hope, embodies the very tensions Kabbalah describes. The stage becomes a mirror of ascent, where every choice carries both peril and the promise of illumination.

*Household Gods* carries the same current, though in a subtler form. Instead of mythic pilgrimage, the setting is the ordinary home. Yet here, too, the Kabbalistic vision emerges: the clash between daily habit and the pull of higher ideals reflects the belief that divinity pervades all levels of life. Crowley uses wit and satire to show that spiritual discovery does not belong only to ritual and legend. It breaks into the common world, in the conversations of neighbors, in the small choices that shape a day.

Taken together, these plays demonstrate Crowley's ability to turn mystical symbolism into living theatre. They are not only stories but reflections of a spiritual map — works that dramatize how the human will moves between desire, destiny, and the search for transcendence. To watch them is to see the architecture of Kabbalah given flesh and voice, inviting the audience to recognize the patterns of their own striving within the drama on the stage.

## Christian Mysticism — Hidden Light and Devotion

Alongside Thelema and Kabbalah, Crowley drew from Christian mystical traditions, especially those emphasizing inner transformation, contemplation, and the presence of the divine in everyday life. Christian mysticism, with its focus on devotion and spiritual ascent, resonated with Crowley's broader philosophical project even as he departed from orthodox religion.

In *Tannhäuser*, Christian mystical motifs shape the story's exploration of spiritual aspiration and redemption. Characters struggle with temptation and sin while longing for transcendence. Their journey reflects the tension between worldly desire and higher purpose. Crowley shows that true illumination is not only intellectual but experiential, arising through personal trials, self-discipline, and the alignment of will with the divine.

*Household Gods* applies these ideas more subtly. Set in a domestic, satirical environment, the play illustrates that the divine can be present in ordinary life. The tension between material preoccupation and the pursuit of higher meaning mirrors the mystical insight that spiritual understanding often resides in mundane routines, waiting to be recognized through attention and effort.

By drawing on Christian mysticism, Crowley enriched his plays with layers of ethical and spiritual reflection. Audiences encounter not only conflict and comedy but also a sense of inner, transformative light guiding choices and shaping challenges. These threads reinforce recurring themes of transformation and the interplay between the worldly and the transcendent, bridging mystical philosophy with dramatic storytelling.

## Recurring Motifs — Transformation and the Tension Between Worlds

Throughout Crowley's plays, certain motifs consistently surface, uniting the philosophical and mystical currents of Thelema, Kabbalah, and Christian mysticism. Chief among these is transformation—the process of change, growth, and awakening that shapes both character and narrative. In the lofty, mythic world of *Tannhäuser* as well as the domestic satire of *Household Gods*, Crowley portrays the struggle to reconcile inner aspiration with outer reality, the spiritual with the everyday.

The tension between worldly desire and transcendent aim recurs in every play. In *Tannhäuser*, characters contend with lust, ambition, and attachment even as they pursue spiritual insight and self-mastery. This interplay reflects the Thelemic call to align one's will with higher purpose and echoes Kabbalistic and mystical notions of ascent. In *Household Gods*, the same tension appears in routine life: social expectation, material preoccupation, and habit clash with the characters' search for meaning, often with humor yet always with depth, showing that transformation need not remain in mystical or heroic realms.

Crowley also emphasizes spiritual aspiration and the pursuit of higher consciousness, dramatized through challenge, choice, and consequence. Symbols, dialogue, and narrative structure reinforce that growth and insight are earned, requiring courage, discernment, and self-discipline, whether the figure is a mythic hero or an ordinary householder.

By weaving these motifs throughout his plays, Crowley makes philosophical and mystical principles visible on stage. Transformation, tension between worlds, and striving toward higher understanding are not abstract theories; they are lived experiences, both for his characters and for the audience who witnesses them. These recurring threads create a thematic coherence that unites his diverse influences and affirms the distinctive voice that defines Crowley's drama.

# AUTHORIAL VISION AND PURPOSE

When Aleister Crowley wrote his plays, he was engaging in more than storytelling. He wanted the stage to show human choices and moral challenges as they unfold in life. He believed theatre could make abstract ideas visible, allowing audiences to witness will and discipline in action. The plays were a way to examine how people confront temptation, struggle with ambition, and seek growth.

Crowley often reflected on this purpose in his journals and letters. In 1907, he wrote that drama is "a mirror for the mind, showing the struggle and triumph of the human spirit in forms the intellect alone cannot touch." In another letter to a student of the A∴A∴, he suggested that performance could awaken reflection and inspire action more effectively than lectures or ritual. His intention was for audiences to see themselves in the drama, and to consider how their own choices reflect their deeper purpose.

The two plays accomplish this in different ways. *Tannhäuser* dramatizes the heroic struggle between desire and higher aspiration. Characters face repeated trials, and the audience observes the consequences of moral and spiritual decisions. Crowley wanted viewers to feel the weight of each choice and to recognize that growth comes from effort and reflection. In contrast, *Household Gods* situates the same ideas in a domestic setting. Humor and everyday interactions illustrate how spiritual insight can emerge in ordinary life. The tension between routine and higher ideals becomes apparent, showing that transformation is possible even in small, mundane moments.

Crowley's broader philosophy, particularly his principle of discovering one's true will, shapes both works. The structure of the plays reflects his belief that effort and self-awareness are necessary for growth. Crowley carefully designed symbolism, dialogue, and plot to make abstract spiritual concepts tangible. By presenting these ideas through drama, he sought to reach audiences in a way that essays or instruction could not.

In *Tannhäuser*, Crowley took a familiar legend and transformed it into an exploration of moral and spiritual challenge. The story follows the hero as he faces temptation repeatedly, each encounter revealing the tension between earthly desire and higher purpose. Rather than simply recounting the legend, Crowley used it as a framework to dramatize the struggle of aligning one's actions with deeper spiritual principles.

The play invites the audience to feel the significance of each choice. Crowley wanted viewers to understand that living according to one's true will requires attention, courage, and effort. Every trial the hero encounters is designed to illustrate the consequences of yielding to temptation or pursuing virtue. The drama makes the abstract idea of moral growth concrete, allowing the audience to witness the effort required to cultivate insight and self-mastery.

Crowley also emphasizes that personal development emerges through engagement with life's challenges rather than through avoidance or passive reflection. The hero's journey demonstrates that understanding and wisdom are earned by confronting difficulties and making deliberate decisions. In this way, the narrative becomes a mirror for the audience, encouraging reflection on the forces shaping their own choices and the values guiding their lives.

By reshaping the legend in this manner, Crowley combines storytelling with philosophical and spiritual instruction. The familiar elements of myth and legend are present, but they serve a larger purpose: to reveal the patterns of desire, discipline, and awakening that define the Thelemic path. *Tannhäuser* is therefore not only a drama to be watched, but also an experience that engages the intellect, imagination, and conscience of the audience.

*Household Gods* brings Crowley's ideas into a domestic, satirical setting. Unlike the mythic and heroic scope of *Tannhäuser*, this play focuses on ordinary life, showing how spiritual and moral challenges appear in the routines of family and society. The pressures of habit, social expectation, and domestic responsibility become the obstacles the characters must navigate in order to gain awareness and insight.

Crowley demonstrates that spiritual understanding does not require grand quests or heroic gestures. Even small interactions, like a conversation between neighbors or a family argument, can reveal the dynamics of desire, choice, and growth. By placing these moments on the stage, he emphasizes that the potential for transformation exists in everyday circumstances. The audience can recognize the patterns of their own lives in these ordinary scenes.

Humor and satire are central to the play's approach. They highlight the contrast between mundane concerns and higher aspirations, making the tension both entertaining and instructive. Crowley uses comedy not to diminish the spiritual themes, but to show that insight can be approached lightly, without the weight of solemn ritual. The sacred, he suggests, can emerge spontaneously in daily life.

Through *Household Gods*, Crowley encourages the audience to observe their surroundings carefully, reflect on the forces influencing their decisions, and act with intention. The play presents a vision of growth that is accessible and practical. It asserts that the pursuit of one's true will is not limited to extraordinary feats or mystical rites, but is woven into the choices and actions of ordinary existence.

The philosophical framework of Thelema is central to both plays. At the heart of Crowley's thought is the principle of discovering and following one's true will, and this idea shapes both character development and narrative structure. The plays are designed to show how effort, choice, and reflection guide individuals toward alignment with their deeper purpose. Crowley's goal was not to lecture or instruct directly, but to embed these principles in the lives and actions of his characters.

The A∴A∴, Crowley's system of disciplined spiritual practice, informs the progression of trials and moral challenges in the plays. Characters are placed in situations that require careful attention, courage, and ethical discernment. The rhythm of challenge, reflection, and reward mirrors the practices he outlined for members of the order, showing that growth is achieved through consistent effort rather than sudden insight.

Kabbalistic symbolism provides a subtle architecture for the inner journey. Imagery drawn from the Tree of Life and other mystical structures shapes the way characters confront desire, temptation, and aspiration. These symbols are never explained outright; they appear naturally in dialogue, setting, and plot, allowing audiences to sense the deeper layers without feeling taught or constrained.

Christian mystical motifs also play a role, emphasizing ethical reflection and the presence of higher guidance. The tension between worldly concerns and spiritual aspiration echoes the contemplative traditions Crowley studied, showing that the pursuit of insight involves both practical engagement and moral awareness. By weaving these influences into the action of the plays, Crowley ensures that philosophical and spiritual ideas are experienced rather than imposed, giving the audience a lived sense of his vision.

Crowley did not expect audiences to grasp every symbolic meaning immediately. He designed his plays as invitations rather than instructions. They were meant to encourage reflection and discussion. Each scene offers opportunities to observe patterns in human behavior, to consider the consequences of choices, and to recognize the ways intention shapes action.

The plays suggest that growth and awareness are not limited to extraordinary or heroic experiences. Even the routines of daily life carry lessons and potential insight. By showing characters navigating ordinary challenges, Crowley highlights the idea that transformation emerges from an attentive engagement with the world around us. The familiar becomes a stage for reflection, revealing layers of meaning that might otherwise go unnoticed.

Crowley's intention was to create theatre that is active rather than passive. He wanted audiences to participate mentally and emotionally, engaging with their own inner journeys while following the narrative. The plays function as mirrors, inviting each observer to consider their values, decisions, and aspirations. This approach transforms the act of watching into a form of personal inquiry.

By blending narrative, symbolism, and reflection, Crowley gives audiences more than entertainment. His work provides a framework for thinking about morality, desire, and spiritual striving, encouraging dialogue and contemplation long after the performance ends. In this way, the theatre becomes both a space for observation and a catalyst for self-examination.

By reading or viewing *Tannhäuser* and *Household Gods* with this perspective, audiences gain a deeper understanding of Crowley's broader project. The plays are not simply entertainment; they examine the nature of will, the challenges of morality, and the processes of personal transformation. Crowley shows that these themes are not confined to extraordinary or mythic events; they also appear in the routines and choices of everyday life.

The plays encourage audiences to pay attention to both the ordinary and the remarkable. Insight can emerge in small moments, and ethical understanding develops through observation and reflection. Crowley presents the sacred as something that permeates daily existence, rather than a distant or inaccessible ideal.

Crowley asks readers and viewers to engage thoughtfully with the material. By observing the characters' decisions and struggles, the audience is invited to consider their own choices. Reflection on the interplay of desire, discipline, and higher purpose becomes a natural part of experiencing the drama, making the plays both instructive and meaningful.

Ultimately, approaching these works with Crowley's purpose in mind enhances appreciation of their depth and intention. The humor, tension, and narrative gain new resonance, and the audience can perceive the careful integration of philosophy, symbolism, and ethical reflection. In this way, the plays offer more than performance; they provide a lens through which to explore the human condition and the pursuit of higher understanding.

# *TANNHÄUSER*

## Synopsis and Background

*Tannhäuser* draws from the medieval German legend of the knight-poet Tannhäuser, a man torn between earthly desire and spiritual aspiration. Crowley's adaptation transforms the familiar myth into a philosophical and mystical exploration, emphasizing the tension between temptation, self-mastery, and the pursuit of one's true will. While Wagner's opera dramatizes romantic and moral struggle in grand musical terms, Crowley's play focuses on the inner life, moral choice, and the hero's psychological and spiritual development.

The story follows Tannhäuser, a gifted and passionate knight, who becomes ensnared by the seductive powers of the Venusberg, the mythical subterranean realm of Venus. There, he experiences indulgence and sensual pleasure, but also recognizes the spiritual cost of unbridled desire. Crowley presents this not as condemnation but as a natural human conflict: the clash between instinct and aspiration, temptation and will.

Haunted by both guilt and longing, Tannhäuser seeks redemption and understanding. His journey becomes a pilgrimage, literal and symbolic, reflecting the Thelemic principle of discovering and following one's true will. Encounters with other characters — representing moral, spiritual, and worldly challenges — shape his growth. Each trial illuminates aspects of human experience: lust, ambition, pride, and the constant need for discernment.

Crowley layers the narrative with mystical symbolism. The Venusberg is not merely a physical location but a representation of the lower self, the unconscious impulses that must be understood and integrated. The pilgrimages and moral dilemmas function as stages of ascent, echoing Kabbalistic and Christian mystical motifs: the struggle to align earthly action with higher purpose, the pursuit of illumination, and the tension between material attachment and spiritual liberation.

By reimagining Tannhäuser, Crowley shifts the emphasis from a tale of moral judgment to a drama of self-realization. The knight's journey becomes a map of human striving, where desire, discipline, and insight intersect. In this light, the play serves both as a story and as a reflective tool, inviting audiences to observe the challenges of choice, the consequences of action, and the possibilities of personal transformation. The legend becomes a stage on which Crowley dramatizes the central Thelemic question: how does one live authentically, in accordance with the deepest currents of the self, while navigating the demands and distractions of the world?

## Composition History and Context

Aleister Crowley wrote *Tannhäuser* around 1907, during a period of intense literary and spiritual activity. This was shortly after his experiences with the Hermetic Order of the Golden Dawn, and during the early development of his own mystical system, the A∴A∴. At this time, Crowley was both consolidating his understanding of ritual magick and experimenting with literary forms that could embody philosophical and mystical principles. The play represents a fusion of his literary ambition and spiritual vision, aiming to bring the insights of Thelema and personal will to the stage.

The tension between Victorian moral conservatism and the burgeoning modernist experimentation in literature and drama marked the literary and theatrical environment of early 20th-century England. Crowley's work reflects both influences: he draws on the symbolist and decadent traditions that explored psychology, desire, and morality, while also responding to the constraints of conventional stagecraft and audience expectations. Unlike many contemporaries, Crowley envisioned drama as a form of ritual: a space where actors and audience could engage with moral, spiritual, and philosophical truths in a living, participatory way.

His influences were eclectic but focused. Wagner's operatic *Tannhäuser* provided a narrative framework and symbolic inspiration, but Crowley reshaped the story to emphasize internal struggle, moral choice, and the ascent toward higher consciousness, rather than musical spectacle or romantic passion. Other literary models included Browning's dramatic monologues, Maeterlinck's symbolist plays, and the mystical allegories of the late 19th-century esoteric revival. Crowley sought to synthesize these strands into a form that could communicate both drama and instruction, blending narrative tension with philosophical depth.

Crowley's goal was not merely to entertain but to offer a stage as a mirror for spiritual reflection. He imagined audiences observing characters as models of action and will, with the hope that they might recognize similar patterns in their own lives. In this sense, *Tannhäuser* functions as both play and ethical experiment: the narrative conveys the consequences of desire and aspiration while dramatizing the steps toward self-realization.

The historical and cultural context is also important. Social comedies, melodramas, and moralistic productions largely dominated England's theatre scene, often avoiding the exploration of mystical, erotic, or controversial themes. Crowley's *Tannhäuser* stood apart from this mainstream: it was dense, symbolic, and intentionally provocative, blending myth, mysticism, and moral philosophy in ways that challenged both conventional audiences and the limits of theatrical form. While it was unlikely to be produced on the commercial stage, it reflected Crowley's ambition to elevate drama into a medium capable of spiritual and intellectual engagement.

In short, *Tannhäuser* emerges from a moment in Crowley's life when his literary, philosophical, and mystical explorations were deeply intertwined. The play illustrates his commitment to integrating life, ritual, and art, using drama as a tool for reflection and ethical inquiry. It is both a product of its time and a work that transcends its era, offering insights into the challenges of desire, moral choice, and self-mastery that remain compelling today.

## Early Reception and Staging

Unlike many of Crowley's contemporaries, *Tannhäuser* was never professionally staged during his lifetime. The play's symbolic density, philosophical ambition, and mystical elements made it a difficult fit for the conventional English theatre of the early 20th century. Crowley himself envisioned the work as more than mere entertainment; he intended it as a kind of living ritual, where actors and audience alike could engage with spiritual and moral truths. In practice, this meant the play was largely read privately or shared among a small circle of disciples and literary peers, rather than performed publicly.

Contemporary responses were therefore limited. Those who encountered the text, often members of the A∴A∴, the O.T.O., or literary-minded friends, recognized its ambitious blend of myth, philosophy, and symbolism. Some admired its depth and audacity, while others found it dense, obscure, or challenging to conventional dramatic expectations. Crowley's reputation as a scandalous figure may also have discouraged mainstream interest; theatres and producers were unlikely to stage work associated with someone widely labeled "the wickedest man in the world."

Despite its lack of professional performance, *Tannhäuser* circulated in manuscript and print form among students of occultism and literary aficionados, earning a measure of quiet admiration. Crowley's dramatization of the inner moral and spiritual struggle often attracted readers, who saw the play as a synthesis of mythic narrative and ethical exploration. Its complex symbolism, rich language, and philosophical depth offered a model of drama that went beyond surface action, inviting audiences, whether in reading or private staging, to reflect on the dynamics of desire, discipline, and moral choice.

In later decades, scholars, literary historians, and practitioners of Thelema revisited the text. Its importance became recognized less as theatre for commercial consumption and more as an artistic and philosophical experiment, a vehicle for demonstrating Crowley's ideals of will, aspiration, and transformation. Modern readers and performers increasingly view the play as a blueprint for ritualized or experimental theatre, where visual, auditory, and symbolic elements converge to embody ethical and mystical concepts. Its historical "failure" to reach the stage is therefore less a mark against its quality and more a reflection of how ahead of its time it was in blending philosophy, mysticism, and drama.

In short, *Tannhäuser* occupies a unique place in Crowley's oeuvre: rarely performed, occasionally read, but consistently regarded as a deeply instructive and symbolic work. Its reception highlights both the limitations of contemporary theatre and the forward-thinking nature of Crowley's vision, showing a play designed not for conventional entertainment but for reflection, insight, and engagement with the human struggle toward self-realization.

## Modern Interpretive Possibilities and Performance Commentary

*Tannhäuser* can be approached by readers and theatre practitioners in ways that bring both its mystical and dramatic dimensions to life. Crowley's symbolic language, moral complexity, and philosophical depth invite creative interpretation, allowing directors and performers to explore the play as both drama and ritual.

One approach is minimalist staging, emphasizing the psychological and spiritual journey of the characters over elaborate sets. The Venusberg, for instance, could be suggested through lighting, sound, and movement rather than literal representation, highlighting the realm as a symbolic space for temptation and desire. The pilgrimage and encounters along

Tannhäuser's journey can be emphasized through choreography, stage design, and atmospheric effects, drawing the audience into the hero's inner struggle.

Crowley's heightened, poetic dialogue presents challenges for performance but also offers opportunities. Actors might approach lines as incantations or meditative statements, allowing the rhythm and intention behind the words to carry meaning beyond conventional speech. In this sense, the play can function as a ceremonial performance, blending theatre with contemplative or reflective practice. Directors can experiment with pacing, pauses, and repetition to evoke the ritualized quality of moral and spiritual choice.

Musical and auditory elements can further enrich interpretation. Though Crowley did not specify a score, the use of ambient music, chant, or symbolic sound motifs can underscore the tension between earthly and transcendent realms. Modern technology: projections, dynamic lighting, or interactive sound design, can amplify the symbolic resonance of each scene, creating a sensory experience that mirrors the hero's psychological and spiritual ascent.

Interpretive focus can also extend to moral and philosophical engagement. Directors and audiences today might emphasize themes of authenticity, discipline, and personal will, connecting Crowley's early 20th-century mystical ideas to contemporary concerns. The tension between desire and higher purpose, central to the Venusberg sequences, can resonate with modern viewers navigating ethical, social, or personal challenges.

For readers and students, *Tannhäuser* offers opportunities for intellectual and spiritual exploration even without performance. Close reading can reveal the interplay of Thelemic principles, Kabbalistic symbolism, and Christian mystical motifs, showing how Crowley structured trials, temptation, and choice as steps toward self-realization. In educational or discussion settings, the play can serve as a springboard for reflection on moral philosophy, mystical practice, and the creative integration of narrative and ritual.

Ultimately, *Tannhäuser* lends itself to flexible, imaginative interpretation. Whether staged as experimental theatre, approached as a reading exercise, or studied for its philosophical content, the play invites audiences to engage actively, considering the consequences of desire, the pursuit of higher aspiration, and the challenges of discovering one's true will. Crowley's vision for the stage, a space for observation, reflection, and spiritual resonance, remains compelling and adaptable, offering modern readers and performers a unique encounter with a text that bridges legend, philosophy, and mystical practice.

## HOUSEHOLD GODS

### Synopsis and Background

*Household Gods* shifts Crowley's focus from mythic heroism to the ordinary world, examining spiritual and moral challenges within a domestic, satirical setting. The play centers on a family navigating daily life, social expectations, and the subtle pressures of routine, showing how desire, ambition, and moral choice appear not only in heroic quests but in ordinary existence.

The central characters are members of a household whose lives are marked by petty conflicts, societal expectations, and recurring personal frustrations. Each character embodies aspects of human nature: ambition tempered by fear, desire entangled with responsibility, and the constant tension between comfort and aspiration. Crowley's satirical touch allows audiences to recognize the humor and folly of daily life, even as the play illustrates profound lessons about self-discipline and moral reflection.

The narrative unfolds through a series of domestic episodes, where ordinary situations: family arguments, social obligations, or personal missteps, become stages for ethical and spiritual insight. Crowley's characters are neither purely virtuous nor irredeemably flawed; they are living examples of the human struggle to align action with deeper purpose. Each trial, whether comic or tense, provides an opportunity for reflection, inviting audiences to see themselves mirrored in the choices and contradictions of the household.

Symbolism in *Household Gods* is subtler than in *Tannhäuser*, yet it remains significant. The household is also where desires, responsibilities, and higher aspirations intersect; therefore, it can be seen as a microcosm of the world. Daily routines, such as cooking, cleaning, conversations, and domestic labor, become allegories of discipline, attention, and ethical engagement, reflecting Thelemic ideas about living according to one's true will in every aspect of life.

Crowley's use of humor and satire distinguishes the play, offering insight without solemnity. The comic elements underscore human folly while simultaneously highlighting the opportunity for growth and reflection embedded in everyday life. Crowley demonstrates that transformation emerges whenever individuals confront desire, duty, and conscience by situating spiritual and philosophical themes within familiar domestic settings.

In essence, *Household Gods* functions as a mirror of ordinary life, showing that the challenges of moral and spiritual development are present in the routines, habits, and relationships that shape daily existence. While *Tannhäuser* dramatizes ascent and heroism, *Household Gods* dramatizes the potential for insight, discipline, and ethical action within the ordinary human sphere, making the play both relatable and instructive for contemporary audiences.

## Composition History and Context

*Household Gods* was written in the 1910s to 1920s, during a period when Aleister Crowley was deeply involved with the A∴A∴ and the O.T.O., and simultaneously producing a wide range of literary works, including plays, poetry, and essays. This period of Crowley's life reflects a maturing of his philosophical and spiritual vision: he had solidified the principles of Thelema, honed his understanding of ritual magick, and gained extensive experience in both travel and literary experimentation. *Household Gods* emerges from this intersection of literary skill, mystical insight, and philosophical purpose, translating abstract principles into a form accessible to audiences familiar with ordinary life.

In contrast to Tannhäuser, which used myth and legend, Household Gods is grounded in the domestic and social world. Crowley wanted to demonstrate that people could apply spiritual principles, especially the pursuit of one's true will, within everyday circumstances, not just through heroic actions, quests or mystical rituals. The play's focus on family life, social pressures, and ordinary routines reflects both a pedagogical intent and a literary experiment: to show that comedy, satire, and subtle drama can carry philosophical and spiritual weight.

Literarily, Crowley was influenced by the symbolist and modernist movements, as well as English social comedy, yet he deliberately subverted conventional stage expectations. While the domestic setting might suggest lighthearted farce, Crowley infused the play with moral tension, ethical reflection, and mystical undertones, encouraging audiences to look beyond surface humor and perceive the deeper currents of desire, discipline, and aspiration. This blending of the mundane with the metaphysical mirrors his broader Thelemic philosophy, which holds that every moment of life is a potential site for aligning with true will.

Historically, the play was unlikely to be staged commercially, partly due to Crowley's controversial reputation and partly because of its unusual combination of domestic realism and esoteric philosophy. Like *Tannhäuser, Household Gods* circulated primarily in manuscript or limited publication, reaching readers within Crowley's networks of disciples, literary contacts, and occult enthusiasts. Despite its limited exposure, the play exemplifies Crowley's belief that everyday life is a stage for moral and spiritual development, translating complex ideas into scenarios that audiences could recognize and relate to.

In essence, *Household Gods* represents Crowley's effort to bring

Thelemic and mystical principles into the domestic sphere, demonstrating that heroic legend or ceremonial ritual does not restrict self-awareness, ethical reflection, and spiritual growth. Its composition reflects both a mature philosophical vision and a playful literary sensibility, revealing Crowley as a writer capable of philosophical depth, social insight, and theatrical innovation within a familiar, approachable framework.

## Early Reception and Staging

*Household Gods* was rarely, if ever, staged during Crowley's lifetime. Its combination of domestic realism, satirical humor, and mystical undertones made it difficult to classify for the mainstream theatre of early 20th-century England. While it avoided the mythic and heroic scope of *Tannhäuser*, the play's philosophical depth and subtle esoteric references still placed it outside conventional commercial drama, which generally favored either light social comedies or moralistic plays with clear resolutions.

Because of this, *Household Gods* circulated primarily in manuscript and limited print editions, reaching a small audience of Crowley's disciples, literary acquaintances, and students of Thelema. Those familiar with his mystical philosophy could appreciate the interplay between domestic farce and ethical reflection, while casual readers might enjoy the humor and social commentary on family dynamics, social expectations, and human folly.

Critical reception in Crowley's time was sparse, largely because the play did not enter mainstream theatrical discourse. Among readers, *Household Gods* was often considered innovative and intellectually ambitious; it blended comedy with moral and spiritual insight. Its subtle use of Thelemic principles, symbolic representation of domestic life, and emphasis on personal growth marked it as a work that required attentive reading or careful staging to fully appreciate.

Modern scholars and performers have increasingly considered *Household Gods* as a template for reflective or experimental theatre. Its domestic and accessible setting allows for creative interpretation: directors can emphasize the humor, the ethical dilemmas, or the mystical undertones, depending on the production's focus. Today, the play also resonates as a study of ordinary life as a site of moral and spiritual engagement. It shows that the pursuit of higher consciousness emerges in the routines and choices of daily existence and is not limited to heroic deeds or mystical visions.

In summary, *Household Gods* shared with *Tannhäuser* the characteristic of being ahead of its time. While commercial theatre largely ignored it. Its enduring value lies in its blend of satire, philosophical reflection, and mystical insight and offers modern readers and performers a rich text for exploring ethical choice, spiritual growth, and the hidden drama of everyday life.

## Modern Interpretive Possibilities and Performance Commentary

Modern readers and theatre practitioners can approach *Household Gods* with a variety of interpretive strategies that highlight its satirical, domestic, and philosophical dimensions. Its focus on ordinary life, humor, and subtle moral reflection makes it highly adaptable for contemporary staging.

One approach is naturalistic staging, emphasizing the domestic setting — kitchens, parlors, or family rooms — to anchor the play in familiar, everyday environments. Simple sets and props can accentuate the realism of the household, allowing audiences to recognize themselves in the characters' routines, conflicts, and small triumphs. Directors can focus on timing, comic beats, and interpersonal dynamics to bring out the play's humor while maintaining the underlying philosophical and moral themes.

Actors might approach dialogue as both comic and reflective, balancing the farcical elements with moments of introspection or ethical significance. Characters' petty quarrels, social anxieties, and domestic mishaps can serve as microcosms of larger spiritual and moral struggles, demonstrating how ethical and aspirational challenges arise in ordinary contexts. This mirrors Crowley's intention: that spiritual insight and personal growth emerge through attentive engagement with daily life.

Modern productions could also incorporate symbolic or ritualistic touches, subtly highlighting the Thelemic and mystical undercurrents without detracting from the domestic realism. Lighting, sound, or minimal props can underscore moments of moral or spiritual tension, reinforcing that even mundane interactions carry significance in the characters' pursuit of self-awareness and alignment with true will.

For readers and students, *Household Gods* offers opportunities for analysis and reflection similar to *Tannhäuser*, but in a more approachable form. Discussion can focus on the ethical choices of characters, the influence of routine and social expectation, and the ways humor reveals both human folly and potential for growth. Its domestic focus allows audiences to draw parallels with their own lives, seeing how personal development and moral reflection unfold in everyday moments.

Ultimately, *Household Gods* is a versatile text for both stage and study. Directors can emphasize comedy, social commentary, or ethical and mystical reflection, creating productions that entertain while provoking thought. Readers can engage with the text as a mirror of daily life, noticing how Crowley's philosophical and spiritual ideas permeate even the most ordinary circumstances. In either medium, the play continues Crowley's mission of demonstrating that transformation, insight, and alignment with one's true will are not reserved for mystical rites but are accessible in the familiar rhythms of everyday life.

# CROWLEY AND THEATRE

Aleister Crowley approached theatre as more than entertainment: he saw it as a living ritual, where drama, symbolism, and human action converged to produce a transformative experience. The stage, for him, was a place where he could make the philosophical, moral, and mystical dimensions of life tangible, and turn abstract ideas into events people could witness, feel, and internalize.

In this view, every play was a kind of magical working. Characters, dialogue, and staging were not merely tools for storytelling; they functioned as vehicles for the projection of will and consciousness. Crowley believed that through careful attention to performance — including gesture, intonation, timing, and spatial relationships — theatre could awaken insight in both actor and audience, creating an environment where inner reflection and transformation were possible.

This ritualized approach reflects the principles of Thelema and the A∴A∴, in which ordinary actions, when imbued with intention and awareness, become spiritual exercises. Just as ceremonial magick turns symbolic acts into processes of self-development, Crowley's theatre transformed dramatic enactment into a means of exploring human will, ethical choice, and spiritual aspiration.

Crowley often emphasized that theatre could operate on multiple levels simultaneously:

Narrative level: a story of human struggle, desire, or conflict.

Symbolic level: representation of mystical or philosophical principles.

Ritual level: enactment as a participatory, transformative experience for all involved.

In his writings, Crowley suggested audiences should not simply watch passively but engage with the performance as if attending a ceremony. This concept makes Crowley's plays highly distinctive: they blur the line between art and magick, theatre and ritual, reflection and experience. The stage transforms into a microcosm of life, where every choice and movement is significant, and both actors and spectators actively explore desire, discipline, and higher purpose.

## Dramatic Influences — Yeats, Maeterlinck, Ibsen, and Shakespeare

Crowley's vision of theatre was informed by his admiration for several key dramatists, whose work inspired him to explore the fusion of symbolism, philosophy, and ritual in his own plays.

William Butler Yeats was particularly influential. Crowley admired Yeats's use of myth, legend, and ritualized structure, seeing in plays like *The Countess Cathleen* the potential for drama to convey moral and mystical ideas. Yeats's approach demonstrated how poetry and symbolism could elevate the stage beyond simple entertainment, creating a space for reflection and spiritual contemplation, which aligned closely with Crowley's own ambitions for theatre.

Maurice Maeterlinck, the Belgian symbolist playwright, contributed another model of influence. Maeterlinck's focus on atmosphere, mood, and inner life — often prioritizing symbolic action over conventional plot — encouraged Crowley to explore psychological and spiritual depth in his characters. The subtlety of Maeterlinck's symbolism offered a blueprint for incorporating esoteric ideas into narrative without overt exposition, a technique Crowley employed in both *Tannhäuser* and *Household Gods*.

Henrik Ibsen influenced Crowley through his realistic exploration of social pressures and ethical dilemmas. Ibsen demonstrated that theatre could probe human psychology and moral complexity, even in domestic settings. Crowley drew on this to show that ethical and spiritual challenges are not confined to myth or legend but appear within ordinary life, a central theme in *Household Gods*.

Finally, Crowley revered Shakespeare for his unmatched integration of poetry, philosophy, and moral inquiry. Shakespeare's ability to illuminate the tension between desire, duty, and conscience inspired Crowley to create characters whose struggles reflected universal patterns of human aspiration, temptation, and ethical decision-making. Shakespearean drama, for Crowley, exemplified the potential of theatre to mirror human consciousness and illuminate the interplay of action and consequence.

By synthesizing these influences, Crowley developed a theatrical approach that combined symbolist subtlety, psychological insight, mythic resonance, and moral inquiry. His plays reflect both his admiration of these masters and his commitment to creating ritualized, transformative experiences on stage, where philosophical and mystical ideas could be lived rather than merely contemplated.

## Crowley vs. Early 20th-Century Modernist Drama — Contrasts and Innovations

While Crowley admired certain dramatists, his theatrical philosophy often diverged sharply from early 20th-century modernist trends. Modernist drama, emerging during the same period, frequently emphasized fragmentation, social critique, psychological realism, and experimentation with form, seeking to challenge traditional narrative structures and reflect the dislocations of contemporary life.

Crowley, by contrast, approached theatre as a ritualized space for moral, spiritual, and philosophical exploration, rather than as a purely social or formal experiment. Whereas modernist playwrights often fragmented plot and dialogue to mirror the alienation and ambiguity of modern experience, Crowley maintained a coherent symbolic and ethical architecture within his plays. Every action, line of dialogue, and stage direction was imbued with intentionality, echoing his belief that life itself is structured by will and consequence.

In terms of subject matter, modernist drama often focused on societal ills, family conflict, or existential crises, while Crowley used drama to explore universal patterns of desire, aspiration, temptation, and transformation. Even in domestic settings like *Household Gods*, the play elevates everyday conflict into a vehicle for ethical and spiritual insight, distinguishing it from purely realist or satirical modernist works.

Crowley's innovation lies in fusing narrative, symbolic resonance, and ritualistic intention. Whereas many modernists sought to unsettle audiences through ambiguity or disjunction, Crowley aimed to engage audiences actively, inviting them not just to observe, but participate mentally in the moral and spiritual journey enacted on stage. This approach treats theatre as both a mirror and a guide, making the performance a dynamic interplay rather than a passive representation.

By positioning drama as a magical, transformative act, Crowley transcended both conventional theatre and certain strands of modernist experimentation. His plays exemplify a unique hybrid: they are symbolically rich, ethically focused, psychologically nuanced, and spiritually instructive, while remaining dramatically engaging and accessible. In this sense, Crowley carved a distinct theatrical path that integrates his philosophical, mystical, and artistic sensibilities, setting his work apart from contemporaneous trends and providing fertile ground for modern interpretation and performance.

## Performance as Magical Act — The Actor as Vessel for Transformation

For Crowley, the act of performance was inherently magical. He believed the theatre could function as a ritual space, where actors, stagecraft, and audience participation converged to produce a transformative effect. Crowley believed that performers could enact moral, philosophical, and spiritual truths, unlike conventional drama where actors may simply "represent" characters.

Each gesture, inflection, and movement was an intentional act, capable of influencing consciousness both onstage and in the audience. Actors, by embodying the ethical dilemmas, mystical tensions, and spiritual striving of the characters, participated in a process of magickal manifestation — enacting the principles of Thelema, the A∴A∴, and Crowley's broader philosophy through their craft.

This concept aligns with Crowley's understanding of ritual in general: ordinary actions, when imbued with focus, discipline, and will, become potent instruments of transformation. On stage, even mundane gestures or dialogues gain significance, turning performance into a living meditation on desire, will, and consequence. Crowley emphasized that this intentionality distinguishes transformative theatre from mere spectacle: it is not enough to recite lines or follow stage directions; the actor must inhabit the ethical and spiritual reality of the moment.

Crowley also saw audience engagement as crucial. Observers were not passive; by witnessing the enactment of moral struggle and spiritual pursuit, they could reflect on their own choices and ethical paths, experiencing a form of indirect participation in the ritual. theatre thus becomes a shared magickal space: actors embody principles, the narrative demonstrates consequences, and audiences engage in contemplation and recognition of the inner journey.

In practical terms, Crowley encouraged performers to approach their roles with self-awareness and a sense of higher purpose. Physicality, vocal tone, and rhythm were all tools for channeling the symbolic and mystical layers of the text. The ultimate goal was to transform both the performer and the audience, and leave a lasting impression of spiritual resonance.

Through this vision, Crowley positioned theatre as a medium for experiential philosophy and applied magick, where the boundaries between life, ritual, and art dissolve. His plays invite modern directors and performers to embrace this approach, recognizing that performance is not merely representation but a conduit for transformation, echoing the broader principles that animate his literary and mystical work.

# CROWLEY'S SYMBOLISM AND LANGUAGE

At first glance, Aleister Crowley's plays can seem complicated, dense, and even mysterious. The mixture of mystical references, philosophical ideas, and symbolic imagery might feel overwhelming. Yet with the right approach, they are surprisingly accessible and meaningful. Crowley did not write to confuse his audience; he wrote to engage them on multiple levels at once, offering both dramatic entertainment and a mirror for personal reflection.

Reading Crowley is less about memorizing esoteric lore and more about learning to see the layers of meaning. He trusted his audience to observe, interpret, and reflect, and he structured his plays to support this process. The challenge is not understanding every reference at once, but rather to notice the patterns; the moments where desire, choice, and consequence intersect.

Crowley's work rewards patient observation. As you read or watch the plays, you begin to see that seemingly exotic or puzzling symbols often correspond to universal experiences: temptation, ambition, struggle, insight, and transformation. Recognizing these patterns allows the plays to speak clearly and powerfully, even when the mystical language is unfamiliar.

## The Three Levels of Symbolism

Crowley's symbols are deliberately multilayered, and operate simultaneously on three interrelated planes: psychological, mythic, and spiritual. Understanding these levels is key to appreciating his artistry and intention.

- **Psychological Level**

On a psychological level, symbols reveal the inner life of characters. Crowley was keenly interested in the workings of human consciousness, and his plays often dramatize internal conflicts, desires, fears, and aspirations. For instance, hesitation before an important decision may symbolize a character's struggle between immediate gratification and long-term purpose, or between ego-driven impulses and the higher self. The audience is invited to see themselves in these moments, reflecting on how similar forces shape their own lives.

- **Mythic Level**

Symbols also function mythically, connecting individual experience to archetypal narratives and universal human stories. In *Tannhäuser*, the hero's repeated confrontations with temptation mirror timeless journeys of trial, loss, and redemption, linking the personal to the universal. Mountains, roads, and journeys, for example, are more than scenery or plot devices; they embody the hero's quest, giving the narrative a resonance that extends beyond any single character. Through these mythic connections, Crowley's plays transform personal struggles into lessons that feel timeless and archetypal.

- **Spiritual / Mystical Level**

Finally, symbols operate on a spiritual or mystical plane. Crowley's interest in Thelema, Kabbalah, and Christian mysticism informs much of his imagery. Light, shadow, ascent, and other recurring motifs often indicate spiritual insight, and the process of awakening to true will. Unlike a textbook, these symbols are woven naturally into the drama and allows the audience to sense their significance without needing prior esoteric knowledge. They turn the stage into a space of reflection and potential transformation, echoing Crowley's view of theatre as a form of ritual.

Together, these three layers make Crowley's symbolism rich, engaging, and alive. A single image can simultaneously reflect a character's psychology, connect to universal myths, and suggest mystical insight. Learning to see these layers allows readers and viewers to experience the depth and coherence of Crowley's vision, appreciating how story, symbol, and philosophy intersect.

## Recurring Symbols in Crowley's Plays

Crowley often returns to certain visual and thematic motifs, which help unify his work and communicate ideas without relying on overt exposition. Understanding these symbols can reveal the psychological, mythic, and spiritual layers embedded in his drama.

- **Light and Shadow**

One of the most pervasive contrasts in Crowley's plays is light and shadow. Light often represents knowledge, insight, or alignment with true will, while shadow embodies ignorance, temptation, or the pull of ego-driven desire. In *Tannhäuser*, moments of illumination frequently coincide with moral or spiritual revelation, signaling that the character has glimpsed a higher truth. Conversely, shadow may fall across a scene to highlight moments of doubt, ethical lapses, or a surrender of oneself to worldly desire. In *Household Gods*, this motif appears in subtler ways: a dimly lit room or the retreat of sunlight may mirror a character's temporary loss of perspective or moral clarity, showing that spiritual awareness is always at play, even in domestic settings.

- **Ascent and the Mountain**

Crowley often uses the motif of climbing or ascending to signify struggle and aspiration. Mountains, hills, or literal steps are not just physical obstacles; they are symbolic tests of character and will. In *Tannhäuser*, the hero's journey up a treacherous path reflects the inner climb toward mastery, self-understanding, and moral insight. The higher the ascent, the more challenging the trial. It creates a visual metaphor for the effort required to live in accordance with true will. Even in the more domestic *Household Gods*, characters "climb" in subtler ways, navigating social pressures, personal ambitions, or ethical dilemmas that require perseverance and reflection.

- **Mirrors and Reflection**

Mirrors appear frequently as symbols of self-examination and moral introspection. Characters may literally confront their reflection, but more often, the mirror is metaphorical. It appears in dialogue, and in choices that echo earlier actions. These moments invite the audience to observe patterns of behavior, recognize contradictions, and reflect on the consequences of action. In Crowley's theatre, mirrors are rarely passive; they actively engage the viewer in the psychological and spiritual drama unfolding onstage.

- **Roads, Paths, and Journeys**

Journeys, whether a road through a forest, a path across a room, or a figurative moral journey, symbolize the ongoing process of choice and ethical navigation. In *Tannhäuser*, the hero's physical travels mirror the moral and spiritual path he must navigate, with each step carrying consequences for his soul and will. In *Household Gods*, the "road" may be a mundane routine or social interaction, but it is no less significant: Crowley demonstrates that even ordinary paths carry the potential for ethical growth and self-realization.

- **The House and Domestic Space**

The motif of the house appears most prominently in *Household Gods*, representing containment, routine, and the ordinary framework of life.

Yet Crowley transforms the domestic space into a site of spiritual and moral testing. The familiar becomes a stage for reflection, where small interactions become opportunities for subtle transformation. Even in *Tannhäuser*, settings such as castles or halls often function as symbolic "houses", containing the hero within structures of desire, temptation, and moral challenge.

- **Music and Sound**

Music recurs as a symbol of harmony, alignment, and emotional resonance, and often bridges the psychological and mystical planes. In *Tannhäuser*, song or chant may signify inner harmony, spiritual attunement, or the call of higher purpose. In domestic settings, subtle musical motifs — footsteps, a clock, or rhythmic dialogue — can create emotional cadence, underscoring tension or resolution, and reminding the audience that every aspect of the environment carries symbolic weight.

Through these recurring symbols, Crowley demonstrates how ordinary and extraordinary elements alike can convey psychological states, mythic resonance, and spiritual significance. Recognizing them allows readers and audiences to follow the invisible threads that unify his work, and makes complex philosophical and mystical concepts tangible and memorable.

## Symbolism in Action: Scenes and Characters

Crowley's symbols are not static; they live in the drama, shaping characters, events, and audience perception. Seeing how symbols function within specific scenes helps readers and viewers experience Crowley's philosophical and mystical ideas in motion.

## Tannhäuser: Trials of Desire and Aspiration

In *Tannhäuser*, the hero repeatedly confronts temptation, each trial layered with psychological, mythic, and spiritual meaning. For example:

- **The Mountain** – Tannhäuser's climb represents the arduous effort required to align with true will. Each ascent mirrors an internal struggle: ambition, desire, and moral choice are interwoven. The audience experiences not just the physical climb, but the emotional and spiritual weight of the journey.

- **Light and Shadow** – When the hero glimpses insight or divine guidance, a stage light or symbolic illumination signals awakening or moral clarity. Conversely, darkness often marks moments of lapse, doubt, or surrender to earthly temptation, visually reinforcing the narrative's spiritual stakes.

- **Mirrors and Reflection** – Tannhäuser frequently encounters situations that reflect his past actions or choices, inviting self-awareness and ethical consideration. These reflective moments dramatize the internal consequences of decision-making, showing that growth requires both observation and action.

Crowley's use of these symbols transforms mythic narrative into active philosophical inquiry. The audience witnesses not only the story of a hero but also the patterns of will, struggle, and insight that mirror their own lives.


### Household Gods: Spiritual Striving in Daily Life

In *Household Gods*, symbols operate in subtler, domestic forms, showing that the extraordinary exists within the ordinary:

- **The House** – The setting itself is a crucible for transformation. Characters navigate social pressures, routine, and personal ambition, all within the seemingly mundane confines of home. Every hallway, doorway, and room becomes a space for reflection and ethical choice.

- **The Road and Path** – Even small journeys are imbued with symbolic weight. They map the characters' moral and spiritual progression, illustrating Crowley's principle that transformation occurs through attention and intentional action, not only heroic quests.

- **Light, Shadow, and Music** – These symbols underscore mood and insight. A conversation by candlelight may reveal inner tension, while rhythmic dialogue or subtle musical cues accentuate emotional or ethical undercurrents, engaging the audience in both comedy and contemplation.

Crowley demonstrates that spiritual and ethical insight is not confined to mythic or heroic spaces. By embedding symbolic meaning in the texture of ordinary life, he allows audiences to recognize that moral growth and self-awareness are accessible in every interaction and choice.

### Characters as Living Symbols

Across both plays, the characters themselves embody symbolic significance:

- **Tannhäuser** – Heroic struggle, aspiration, and the tension between desire and higher purpose.
Secondary Figures – Represent specific psychological traits, ethical challenges, or societal pressures. In Tannhäuser, they may appear as

temptresses, guides, or rivals; in Household Gods, they take on familial or social roles that reflect common human conflicts and opportunities for growth.

- **Ensemble Interactions** – Crowley often stages interactions so that the symbolic resonance spreads across the cast, showing how personal choices ripple through relationships, communities, and ethical frameworks.

By observing how symbols unfold through characters, plot, and setting, readers gain a sense of Crowley's unique theatrical philosophy: that life, desire, and spiritual striving are inseparable, and that drama can make abstract ideas tangible, visible, and emotionally immediate.

## Crowley's Language and Dialogue

Crowley's language is as symbolically charged as his imagery, and understanding his dialogue is essential to appreciating the layers of meaning in his plays. He blends poetic diction, ritual cadence, and dramatic realism to create speech that functions on multiple levels. Language, for Crowley, is not merely expression but enactment: a tool of transformation woven directly into dramatic form.

## Poetic and Ritualistic Cadence

Crowley often writes dialogue with a rhythm reminiscent of ritual or incantation. In *Tannhäuser*, speech may rise and fall like a chant, emphasizing moral weight or spiritual significance. Repetition, parallel structure, and heightened phrasing transform ordinary conversation into performative moments of reflection, inviting the audience to engage attentively with ethical and mystical dimensions. These cadences echo his belief in theatre as ritual: words themselves become tools of transformation, shaping consciousness as much as they convey narrative information.

## Character Specific Speech Patterns

Each character's dialogue reflects their psychological and symbolic role. The hero may speak with elevated, reflective language that mirrors internal struggle and aspiration. Secondary characters often have contrasting speech patterns: comedic, abrupt, or mundane dialogue can highlight the ordinary pressures of life, while enigmatic or poetic speech signals guidance, temptation, or spiritual presence. This interplay allows audiences to grasp characters' roles not just through action, but through the texture and tone of speech.

## Word Choice and Symbolic Density

Crowley selects words with precision, often layering multiple meanings or resonances into a single line. For instance, references to "light," "shadow," "path," or "mirror" may serve simultaneously as plot device, psychological insight, and mystical symbol. Understanding these choices enriches the reading experience, and reveals how even simple dialogue can mirror larger philosophical or spiritual truths.

## Humor, Satire, and Subtlety

In *Household Gods*, Crowley's dialogue demonstrates wit and satirical timing, and reflects the play's domestic setting and lighter tone. Even in moments of comedy, language carries symbolic weight: playful banter may illuminate social pressures, ethical conflicts, or moral growth. Humor becomes a conduit for reflection, showing that insight and transformation can emerge through levity as much as through gravitas.

## The Reader and Audience as Participants

Crowley's dialogue often directly or indirectly engages the audience, breaking conventional barriers between stage and observer. Subtle cues, double meanings, and symbolic phrasing invite readers or viewers to think alongside the characters, noticing patterns and reflecting on their own responses. This aligns with his vision of theatre as ritual: the audience is not passive, but a participant in moral, psychological, and spiritual engagement.

By examining Crowley's language carefully, readers gain insight into how his plays function as living, symbolic systems. Every line carries potential significance, every cadence suggests deeper patterns, and every interaction between words and symbols creates a layered, immersive experience that reflects both human reality and spiritual aspiration.

# CROWLEY'S DRAMATIC STRUCTURE AND STAGECRAFT

Crowley's approach to dramatic structure reflects his dual goals of storytelling and spiritual demonstration. Unlike conventional plays that prioritize plot alone, his dramas integrate symbolic architecture, character arcs, and temporal rhythm to create layers of meaning visible both on the page and on the stage. Understanding his structural choices helps readers and audiences appreciate how action, imagery, and philosophy converge in his work.

Crowley often structures his plays so that each scene contributes to multiple levels of development. In *Tannhäuser,* the hero's journey is simultaneously:

- Narrative: advancing the story through trials, encounters, and resolution.

- Psychological: revealing the inner struggles, temptations, and growth of characters.

- Spiritual: illustrating the ascent toward clarity, insight, and alignment with true will.

This layering ensures that audiences are constantly aware of the stakes, both for the characters and for the larger philosophical or mystical lessons the drama embodies. Even seemingly minor episodes contribute to cumulative understanding, echoing Crowley's belief that every moment of life, like every scene on stage, can carry transformative significance.

Repetition is a hallmark of Crowley's structural technique. Key symbols, lines, or situations recur, but each repetition introduces variation. For example, a temptation or challenge may appear multiple times in *Tannhäuser*, each iteration increasing in intensity or presenting a subtle ethical or psychological nuance. This method mirrors ritual practice, emphasizing refinement, reflection, and learning through experience rather than sudden revelation.

Crowley often treats each scene as a microcosm of the play's larger themes. In *Household Gods*, a simple domestic interaction can encapsulate conflict between routine and higher aspiration. It shows how everyday life itself becomes the stage for moral and spiritual growth. By focusing attention on small, self-contained episodes, Crowley demonstrates that transformation is accessible in ordinary circumstances, not just in mythic or heroic contexts.

Physical staging, setting, and props are integral to Crowley's symbolism. Mountains, houses, mirrors, and lighting are not just scenic elements; they function as active participants in the drama, guiding perception and reinforcing the symbolic layers. Strategic lighting, entrances and exits, and positioning of characters reflect the flow of moral and spiritual energy, directing audience attention to crucial moments of insight, struggle, or decision.

Crowley carefully considers the rhythm of action, balancing tension, reflection, and release. Pauses, humor, or domestic scenes intersperse moments of heightened drama, which allows the audience to process symbolic meaning and reflect on ethical or mystical implications. This temporal design reinforces that the audience experiences theatre as both contemplative and transformative, cultivating attention and awareness over time.

Ultimately, Crowley's structural choices serve a larger purpose: to embed philosophical and mystical principles directly into the action of the play. Narrative events, character arcs, and stagecraft all work together to make abstract ideas visibly tangible. The structure itself becomes an extension of his vision of theatre as ritual, demonstrating that form, content, and symbolism are inseparable in the experience of his work.

Crowley's plays, though written in the early 20th century, offer rich opportunities for contemporary staging. Their blend of philosophical depth, symbolic imagery, and dramatic tension allows directors and actors to explore multiple layers of meaning, emphasizing both psychological realism and mystical resonance.

Crowley's works are highly adaptable. *Tannhäuser*, with its mythic and heroic scope, can be staged as a classical, almost operatic drama, emphasizing grandeur, ritual, and spectacle, or it can be modernized, highlighting universal human struggles against desire, ambition, and ethical challenge. *Household Gods*, with its domestic satire, lends itself to intimate productions, where small gestures, nuanced timing, and subtle visual cues carry symbolic weight. This flexibility demonstrates Crowley's understanding that the essence of drama lies in human action and choice, rather than fixed staging conventions.

Directors can highlight Crowley's vision of theatre as ritual by infusing movement, lighting, and sound with symbolic intent. Repeated actions, choreographed gestures, or ritualistic sequences underscore the magical dimension of performance, where actor, character, and audience participate in a transformative process. This approach encourages viewers to experience ethical and spiritual tension rather than simply witnessing a story unfold.

Contemporary productions might explore:

- Psychological realism – focusing on the inner life of characters, showing how desire, moral choice, and ambition create tension and growth.

- Symbolic abstraction – emphasizing visual, auditory, or move-

237

ment-based symbolism to convey mystical or philosophical ideas.

- Satirical and comedic elements – especially in *Household Gods*, where humor and domestic absurdity reveal ethical and spiritual truths.

By blending these approaches, directors can make Crowley's complex themes accessible and compelling for modern audiences.

For Crowley, performance is itself a magical act. Actors embody not just characters, but symbolic forces, ethical dilemmas, and spiritual principles. By committing fully to these roles, performers become conduits for audience reflection, illustrating Crowley's belief that theatre can activate consciousness and inspire self-examination. This transforms the stage into a space where psychological insight and moral inquiry occur in real time, engaging both performer and spectator.

Crowley's plays invite active, thoughtful engagement. Modern productions can emphasize audience participation on a cognitive or emotional level, encouraging viewers to recognize patterns in behavior, moral consequences, and symbolic resonance. By doing so, the plays function not merely as entertainment, but as tools for reflection and insight, fulfilling Crowley's vision of theatre as both ritual and art.

While rich in symbolic and philosophical content, Crowley's plays pose challenges for contemporary performance: archaic diction, mythic references, and complex symbolism can seem dense. However, careful direction, imaginative staging, and thoughtful adaptation can transform these elements into immersive, resonant experiences, demonstrating the enduring relevance and power of his work.

# CROWLEY IN CONTEXT

Aleister Crowley's plays occupy a unique position at the crossroads of several literary currents, reflecting the complex cultural and artistic milieu of the early twentieth century. Around the turn of the 20th century, writers and dramatists were exploring new psychological insights, shifting social mores, and experimental forms of expression. Audiences were beginning to encounter works that challenged conventional morality, questioned the nature of consciousness, and redefined the possibilities of theatrical storytelling.

Crowley was very much a part of this cultural milieu, yet he charted his own singular course. While many contemporaries were negotiating these changes within the bounds of literary fashion or social expectation, Crowley integrated philosophy, mysticism, and ritual directly into his dramatic work. His plays are not merely stories or entertainment; they are staged explorations of will, morality, and spiritual striving, infused with symbolic architecture drawn from Thelema, Kabbalah, and Christian mysticism.

In this context, one can see Crowley as both a participant and an outlier. Like W.B. Yeats, he blended literary artistry with esoteric and symbolic systems; like Oscar Wilde, he courted scandal and challenged social norms; yet unlike either, he treated theatre itself as a medium for transformation, where performance was both artistic expression and ritualized enactment. Understanding the Edwardian and early modern literary environment helps the reader see how Crowley's work fits into broader trends, and how it deliberately pushes against them, anticipating aspects of modernist, existential, and psychological drama.

## Connections to Contemporary Dramatists

Crowley's theatrical sensibilities share notable affinities with major figures of his era, yet his work remains unmistakably singular. Like W.B. Yeats, Crowley understood drama as more than entertainment; it could be ritualized and symbolic, a vehicle for spiritual and psychological exploration. Yeats' early plays, such as *The Countess Cathleen*, emphasize archetypal struggles and mythic resonance, a quality mirrored in the heroic and moral architecture of *Tannhäuser*. Whereas Yeats often drew upon Irish myth and folklore, Crowley's symbolic universe is far more syncretic, weaving together Kabbalah, Thelema, Christian mysticism, and his own personal mythology into a coherent dramatic vision.

Crowley also admired Oscar Wilde for his wit, satire, and incisive social critique, qualities that surface prominently in *Household Gods*. Like Wilde, Crowley exposes social hypocrisy through humor, irony, and dialogue, but his satire often carries an additional layer of mystical and ethical significance, linking domestic absurdity to spiritual principles. In this way, the ordinary setting becomes a stage for observing both moral and spiritual tension.

George Bernard Shaw's influence is apparent in Crowley's interest in ethical dilemmas, social consequence, and the careful observation of human behavior. Shaw's plays frequently probe societal norms and the consequences of personal choice, anticipating Crowley's fascination with moral consequence. Crowley adopts a similar analytical lens, but he frames these concerns through ritualized and spiritually heightened action, rather than through overt social didacticism.

Maurice Maeterlinck, the Belgian Symbolist, similarly resonates in Crowley's attention to fate, destiny, and unseen forces. *Tannhäuser* particularly reflects a Maeterlinckian concern with inner struggle and metaphysical tension, yet Crowley's drama is more overtly didactic, illustrating the principles of will, discipline, and self-mastery central to Thelema.

Finally, Crowley's work reflects a deep engagement with Shakespeare. His use of archetype, elevated language, and moral tension demonstrates an awareness of classical tragedy. Characters face dilemmas reminiscent of Shakespearean drama, where the consequences of desire and action are foregrounded. Yet Crowley diverges in a key way: he explicitly connects inner moral and spiritual development to outward action, transforming tragedy into a staged mirror of spiritual aspiration rather than mere dramatic spectacle.

## Divergences from Mainstream theatre

Although Crowley shared certain thematic interests with his contemporaries, his plays diverge in several striking and deliberate ways. One of the most notable differences is his integration of mysticism. While most Edwardian dramatists remained firmly grounded in human or social psychology, Crowley wove occult and mystical frameworks directly into plot, character, and dialogue. His plays are simultaneously allegorical and instructive, presenting spiritual principles as living drama rather than abstract treatises. In *Tannhäuser*, for example, the hero's trials are not merely narrative tension; they are structured enactments of moral and spiritual ascent, reflecting the principles of Thelema and Kabbalah.

Another distinction is Crowley's philosophical didacticism. Whereas contemporaries often relied on subtle or implicit moral commentary, Crowley's work is consciously educative. Characters embody ethical and spiritual concepts such as True Will, self-mastery, and the consequences of choice. The audience is encouraged to observe these patterns, reflect on them, and recognize their resonance in personal life. Even his humor in

*Household Gods* carries a subtle pedagogical purpose: domestic absurdity becomes a mirror for spiritual insight.

Perhaps most radically, Crowley conceived the stage itself as a ritual space. For him, theatre was not merely a medium for art or social critique; performance could enact transformation for actors, characters, and audience alike. The dramaturgy of his plays is designed to move participants toward reflection, awareness, and moral engagement, creating an experience that blends aesthetic pleasure with the consciousness-expanding goals of ceremonial magick. This conception sets him apart from early 20th-century dramatists, whose primary aim was often to entertain, provoke thought, or critique society, without attempting direct spiritual or psychological transformation.

Through these divergences, Crowley establishes a theatrical mode that is uniquely his own: a fusion of mysticism, philosophy, and ritual, where drama serves as both mirror and guide for the human spirit. His plays are at once entertaining, instructive, and transformative — a radical departure from the norms of Edwardian theatre.

## Position within Literary Movements

Aleister Crowley's plays occupy a unique position at the crossroads of several literary currents, reflecting the complex cultural and artistic milieu of the late Victorian, Edwardian, and early modern periods. One significant influence is Symbolism. Through imagery, archetype, and ritualized action, Crowley aligns with the European Symbolist movement, which sought to represent invisible realities and inner life rather than mere external appearances. Like the Symbolists, he uses stagecraft to evoke psychological and spiritual states, allowing the audience to experience patterns of desire, will, and transformation rather than simply observe narrative events.

At the same time, Crowley shares with the Decadents and the Aesthetic movement—particularly Oscar Wilde—a fascination with beauty, transgression, and intense aesthetic experience. His attention to language, form, and ceremonial detail reflects a deep investment in the artistry of performance, while the thematic focus on moral tension and social convention echoes the preoccupations of fin-de-siècle writers. Even in his domestic satire *Household Gods*, one can detect a Decadent appreciation for irony, wit, and the subtle interplay of desire, propriety, and ethical principle.

Crowley's work also anticipates early modernist concerns. His focus on the will, consciousness, and the psychological dimensions of action prefigures themes that would later be central to modernist drama, from the existential questioning of character motivation to the exploration of ethical and spiritual dilemmas. In this sense, Crowley's plays act as a bridge: they are both rooted in the symbolic and aesthetic traditions of the 19th century and point toward the experimental, introspective theatre of the 20th.

In short, although Crowley is often dismissed as an eccentric occultist operating on the margins, his plays engage seriously and intelligently with the literary currents of his time. They converse with contemporaries, echoing and sometimes amplifying the Symbolist, Decadent, and early modernist impulses in theatre, while also asserting a distinctive synthesis of art, philosophy, and ritual. Crowley's stage is not merely a site of entertainment; it is a space where literary innovation, mystical exploration, and ethical reflection converge.

# CROWLEY AND THE ROOTS OF PSYCHOLOGICAL AND EXISTENTIAL DRAMA

Aleister Crowley's plays anticipate important developments in 20th-century drama, particularly in their focus on psychology, consciousness, and existential choice. Long before modernist and existential playwrights gained prominence, Crowley was staging the inner life of characters as a battleground, where desire, will, and ethical responsibility intersect.

## Focus on Consciousness and Will

Crowley's drama emphasizes the idea that inner will and self-awareness are inseparable from human action. His characters are not simply products of circumstance, social role, or inherited fate; their struggles illuminate the tension between desire and purpose, between habit and aspiration. This emphasis on the conscious shaping of life anticipates both the psychological realism of writers like Eugene O'Neill, who dissected inner conflict and moral ambiguity, and the existential drama of Jean-Paul

Sartre or Albert Camus, which probes freedom, responsibility, and the anxiety inherent in human choice.

In *Tannhäuser*, the hero's repeated confrontations with temptation dramatize the effort required to align with one's true will. Each failure, each partial success, maps an inner process, a psychological journey made visible for the audience. Where later modernist drama might achieve similar insight through fragmented narrative, stream-of-consciousness, or monologue, Crowley makes it embodied and theatrical, showing the stakes of moral and spiritual decision in action.

*Household Gods* brings this approach into the mundane, domestic sphere, demonstrating that ethical and spiritual challenges are not confined to heroic or mythic narratives. The ordinary routines, social expectations, and familial tensions reveal the same inner conflicts Crowley dramatizes on a larger, more symbolic scale in *Tannhäuser*. In doing so, he foreshadows mid-20th-century theatre's fascination with the psychology of everyday life, where even small choices carry existential weight.

By foregrounding consciousness, will, and ethical engagement, Crowley positions his drama at the intersection of the symbolic, mystical, and psychological — an early exploration of terrain that modernist and existential playwrights would later navigate more fully. His work shows that spiritual and moral stakes can be both immediate and universal, whether played out on a mythic stage or in the living room of an ordinary household.

## Ethical and Existential Tension

A hallmark of Crowley's drama is the way characters are placed in situations that illuminate freedom, choice, and consequence. Unlike conventional morality plays, which often present clear distinctions between right and wrong, Crowley's work emphasizes the necessity of conscious decision-making and the weight of personal responsibility. His characters are agents of their own development, reflecting existentialist concerns before they became central to modern theatre.

This approach introduces a deliberate ambiguity into the moral and spiritual landscape of the plays. Rather than offering easy resolutions, Crowley invites the audience to grapple with complexity, observing the characters' struggles and reflecting on the interplay of competing motivations. In *Tannhäuser*, the hero repeatedly faces temptations that test his moral and spiritual discipline, showing how even partial successes or failures carry meaningful consequences. Similarly, in *Household Gods*, the pressures of domestic life become arenas for ethical reflection. Even seemingly mundane actions are imbued with significance, revealing the ethical dimensions of ordinary choices.

Underlying these ethical dilemmas is the principle of self-mastery, a cornerstone of Crowley's Thelemic philosophy. Characters are challenged to discern and enact their true will, developing the inner discipline and awareness necessary for moral and spiritual growth. This internalized struggle is not didactic; rather, it models a form of ethical engagement that requires attention, courage, and reflection. The audience witnesses these processes unfold, gaining insight into the complexity of aligning one's actions with one's deeper purpose.

By foregrounding agency, ambiguity, and self-mastery, Crowley transforms his plays into stages for existential and ethical inquiry. They dramatize the human experience as a continuous negotiation between desire, responsibility, and aspiration, anticipating themes later central to existential drama and psychological theatre. In doing so, Crowley presents a vision of human life in which freedom and consequence are inseparable, and moral development is a lived, ongoing process rather than a series of prescribed rules.

## Anticipation of Modern Psychological Techniques

Crowley's plays exhibit a remarkable sensitivity to the interior life of his characters, foreshadowing dramatic techniques that would only gain widespread attention decades later. His work foregrounds motivation, introspection, and moral conflict, making the inner workings of consciousness a central theatrical concern.

In many passages, dialogue and stage directions function like interior monologues, revealing thought processes, temptation, and reflection. Characters speak and act in ways that allow the audience to perceive the subtle workings of desire, doubt, and ethical deliberation. Even when not explicitly framed as soliloquy, the text invites spectators to witness the unfolding psychological landscape, offering insight into what later dramatists such as Eugene O'Neill or the expressionists would explore through more overt introspective devices.

Crowley also makes extensive use of symbolic action to externalize internal states. Mirrors, thresholds, mountains, and other stage props are more than scenery; they reflect the inner struggles of the characters, translating psychological tension into visual and performative terms. These externalized symbols heighten the audience's perception of desire, fear, and aspiration, a method reminiscent of expressionist theatre where the stage itself embodies psychological reality.

Finally, Crowley heightens dramatic tension through the ethical consequences of choice. Every action carries stakes that reverberate through both the character's inner life and the broader narrative, intensifying awareness of internal conflict. The audience observes not only the external outcome but also the psychological pressure created by these decisions, making moral and spiritual stakes palpable.

Through these techniques, Crowley anticipates many modern innovations in psychological drama, marrying interior reflection with symbolic staging and moral consequence. His plays invite the audience into the minds of the characters, allowing spectators to experience the pressures, doubts, and decisions that define human consciousness — long before such methods became widely recognized in mainstream theatre.

## Bridging Mythic and Domestic

A distinctive feature of Crowley's drama is his ability to translate psychological and existential struggle across scales, from the mythic to the everyday. In *Tannhäuser*, the hero's journey unfolds on a heroic, cosmic stage, filled with legendary trials, temptations, and archetypal figures. Yet even in this elevated setting, the drama is intimately concerned with personal desire, will, and ethical discernment. The audience witnesses not just external conflict, but the inner workings of a mind striving to align with higher purpose.

In contrast, *Household Gods* brings these same dynamics into a domestic and social context. The pressures of routine, family obligations, and social expectation replace mountains and mythic trials, but the underlying tension remains: characters must navigate desire, duty, and aspiration, making choices that reveal moral and spiritual growth. Crowley demonstrates that existential tension is not confined to epic narratives; it is present in ordinary life, and the same attentiveness, courage, and self-mastery apply to small, everyday decisions as they do to heroic deeds.

By bridging these scales, Crowley emphasizes a continuity between the grand and the mundane. Whether on a mythic stage or in a living room, the same principles of conscious choice, moral responsibility, and self-realization operate. This approach allows audiences to see themselves reflected in both heroic and ordinary figures, reinforcing the universality of ethical and spiritual striving. Crowley's drama thus transforms the stage into a space where mythic and domestic experiences converge, showing that the pursuit of awareness, virtue, and purpose is a concern at every level of human life.

## Influence on Later Psychological and Existential Drama

Crowley's plays foreshadow many developments in mid- and late-20th-century theatre. His focus on the inner life of characters, on moral and spiritual freedom, and on the symbolic representation of consciousness anticipated techniques and concerns that would later define expressionist, avant-garde, and existential drama.

In Crowley's work, the stage becomes a site where interior states are made visible, long before psychological and experimental dramatists formalized these methods. The moral and spiritual stakes of each character's choices are rendered not only through dialogue, but through symbolic action, setting, and ritualized structure, creating a drama in which inner conflict and ethical tension are as tangible as any physical confrontation.

Post-war drama, with its attention to ethical ambiguity, choice, and the weight of personal responsibility, resonates strongly with Crowley's concerns. In plays by Eugene O'Neill, Arthur Miller, and Samuel Beckett, characters struggle with desire, failure, and self-awareness, negotiating consequences that shape both their inner and outer worlds. These thematic explorations of human consciousness and moral responsibility echo the structures Crowley had already been employing decades earlier.

In essence, Crowley's plays form a bridge between Edwardian Symbolism and modern psychological drama. They combine ritualized action, symbolic myth, and deep attention to the inner life, while emphasizing the ethical and spiritual dimensions of human choice. His preoccupation with will, consciousness, and moral consequence ensures that the plays remain relevant and insightful for modern readers and performers. Crowley, in this way, explored the enduring questions of human experience long before these ideas entered mainstream theatre, making him a proto-existential dramatist.

# CROWLEY'S INFLUENCE ON COUNTERCULTURE, ART, AND MUSIC

The ideas, persona, and work Crowley left behind exerted a profound and lasting influence on countercultural movements, artistic experimentation, and music. Crowley embodied a spirit of radical individuality, fearless inquiry, and the breaking of societal norms, qualities that resonated strongly with later generations seeking alternatives to conventional morality and restrictive cultural frameworks.

In many ways, Crowley's appeal was as much symbolic as literal. The image of the magician, philosopher, and provocateur became a kind of cultural shorthand for rebellion, curiosity, and spiritual exploration. Artists and musicians drew inspiration from this figure, whether in adopting his imagery, referencing his ideas, or exploring the mystical and philosophical currents he had synthesized in his writing. Crowley's influence was not limited to occultists; it extended to anyone drawn to the tension between freedom and discipline, creativity and ritual, the visible and invisible dimensions of human experience.

His plays offered a model of theatre as experimentation, where symbolism, ritual, and psychological exploration intersected. This concept reverberated through later performance art and avant-garde theatre, where the stage itself could become a laboratory for transformation, reflection, and boundary-pushing expression. Crowley's thought encouraged artists to consider the stage as a site of moral, spiritual, and psychological investigation, rather than only entertainment or social critique.

By situating his work in this context, readers can better understand how Crowley's writings and plays extended far beyond his immediate milieu. They provided a touchstone for artistic and cultural experimentation, a challenge to conventional aesthetics, and a blueprint for integrating philosophy, ritual, and self-expression into creative work. In short, Crowley's legacy in counterculture, art, and music is less about literal performance and more about the enduring influence of his vision of art as a transformative, spiritual, and radical act.

## Crowley as a Cultural Icon

Aleister Crowley's life, adventurous, scandalous, and fiercely intellectual, became a symbol of rebellion and individualism long after his death. The "wickedest man in the world" persona, while often sensationalized, served a paradoxical purpose: it drew attention to his ideas, magnified his influence, and created a template for later generations fascinated by freedom, transgression, and self-realization. Crowley's notoriety, rather than diminishing his impact, amplified his cultural presence, turning him into a figure whose life itself seemed to embody the principles he explored in philosophy, ritual, and theatre.

Writers, artists, and musicians throughout the 20th century found in Crowley a touchstone for creative audacity and spiritual curiosity. Beat poets admired his fearless questioning of society's rules and the pursuit of higher consciousness. Punk and rock musicians embraced his image as an emblem of rebellion, individual will, and occult mystique. Crowley's emphasis on personal responsibility, self-discipline, and alignment with one's true will offered a philosophical depth behind the flamboyant persona, allowing his iconography to resonate beyond simple shock value.

What makes Crowley particularly compelling as a cultural symbol is that he combined intellectual rigor with daring performance. He did not simply live scandalously; he wove philosophy, ritual, and artistic experimentation into the fabric of his life, turning personal choices into a form of dramatic expression. This fusion of art, mysticism, and audacious living provided a model for creative figures seeking ways to merge life, work, and ideology, a model that reverberates through countercultural and avant-garde movements to this day.

By understanding Crowley as a cultural icon, readers can see how his influence extends far beyond the occult or the stage, touching literature, music, art, and performance in ways that celebrate freedom, experimentation, and the bold exploration of human potential.

## Influence on Literature and Theatre

Despite the rare staging of Aleister Crowley's plays, they spread their ideas and symbolic vocabulary extensively in literary and occult circles, subtly influencing the work of later writers and dramatists. Crowley's fusion of mystical concepts with human psychology created a new dramatic approach: characters were not merely social figures or archetypes, but embodiments of inner conflict, ethical tension, and spiritual aspiration. This combination of the personal, the philosophical, and the symbolic offered a model for writers who sought to translate interior life into dramatic action.

One notable impact of Crowley's work lies in the integration of mystical ideas into narrative and stagecraft. Tannhäuser and Household Gods illustrate how spiritual and moral concerns can drive plot, character development, and dialogue. Later avant-garde and expressionist dramatists, working in the mid-20th century, explored similar techniques: internal states made visible, ethical ambiguity foregrounded, and ritualized or symbolic actions forming the backbone of the drama. Crowley's plays can be seen as early experiments in this mode, offering a bridge between Edwardian symbolism and modernist theatre.

Crowley also innovated in symbolic action as a narrative device. The use of mirrors, thresholds, mountains, and domestic spaces as extensions of the characters' inner lives anticipates techniques that became hallmarks of experimental and expressionist theatre. Such devices allowed playwrights to externalize psychology, making abstract states of mind tangible for audiences, and encouraged the exploration of non-linear storytelling and allegorical layering in later drama.

Finally, Crowley's blending of humor, satire, and philosophical reflection, particularly in Household Gods, prefigures the rise of domestic absurdity and black comedy. His ability to embed profound moral and spiritual questions within everyday routines created a model for dramatists who sought to reveal the extraordinary in the ordinary. This demonstrated that heroic or mythic settings need not contain profound ethical and existential dilemmas.

In short, Crowley's literary and theatrical contributions lie less in performance history than in the conceptual and symbolic tools he developed—tools that resonated with later writers eager to experiment with consciousness, morality, and the stage as a space for philosophical exploration.

## Music and the Occult Imagination

Aleister Crowley's influence extended far beyond literature and theatre, reaching deeply into popular culture, particularly music. His persona as the provocative, boundary-breaking mystic resonated with artists who sought to challenge convention, explore spirituality, and fuse ritual with performance. Crowley's fascination with symbolism, personal transformation, and the occult offered a rich imaginative framework for musicians experimenting with new sounds, theatricality, and conceptual imagery.

In the 1960s and 1970s, rock and psychedelic artists were among the first to engage with Crowley's ideas. Jimmy Page of Led Zeppelin, for example, famously collected Crowley-related texts and owned Boleskine House, the former residence of Crowley. Page's interest in ritualized imagery, mystical symbolism, and the integration of mythic narratives into music and album art reflects Crowley's belief in creative expression as a form of magical practice. Similarly, David Bowie explored themes of identity, transformation, and the esoteric, weaving Crowleyan ideas into performances and personas that challenged social norms and engaged audiences in imaginative, almost ritualistic ways.

Crowley's presence also appears in more explicit forms. Ozzy Osbourne's 1980 song "Mr. Crowley" brought his name and reputation to a mainstream audience, cementing his image as a figure of dark fascination, spiritual rebellion, and enigmatic charisma. While the song dramatizes the mythic "wickedest man in the world," it also reflects the enduring cultural magnetism of Crowley's life and ideas, showing how a playwright and mystic of the Edwardian era could captivate audiences across a century.

Beyond these high-profile examples, numerous contemporary and experimental musicians have drawn inspiration from Crowley's integration of ethical, symbolic, and spiritual themes into creative work. From avant-garde composition to theatrical performance in music, Crowley's vision of art as a transformative, almost ritualized act has encouraged generations of artists to treat sound, stagecraft, and performance as vehicles for inner exploration, personal will, and imaginative engagement.

In essence, Crowley's impact on music demonstrates how his ideas transcended their original literary and mystical context. Even if most audiences never encountered his plays firsthand, the spirit of his thought—its blend of discipline, symbolism, and ethical inquiry—permeated the creative imagination, inspiring musicians to experiment boldly and engage deeply with questions of consciousness, transformation, and the occult.

## Countercultural and Artistic Movements

Crowley's ideas found a remarkable resonance with countercultural movements of the 1960s and beyond. His philosophy of True Will—the principle that each person should discover and pursue their authentic purpose—intersected with a growing cultural interest in self-exploration, meditation, and alternative spiritualities. Artists, musicians, and writers saw in Crowley a figure who embodied the pursuit of personal freedom, someone whose life and work encouraged questioning of convention and experimentation with consciousness.

Beyond philosophy, Crowley modeled a life in which creativity and ritual were inseparable. He demonstrated that art could be more than entertainment: it could serve as a form of spiritual practice, a vehicle for personal transformation, and a method of engaging fully with life. Musicians and performance artists, particularly in the psychedelic and avant-garde scenes, drew on this model, using their work not only to express ideas but to enact transformation for themselves and their audiences.

Crowley's plays also illustrated the power of myth, symbolism, and allegory in narrative. The vivid imagery, archetypal conflicts, and mystical structures he employed provided a template for later artists to blend storytelling with symbolic and psychological depth. Visual artists, playwrights, and musicians alike found inspiration in his approach, integrating spiritual and symbolic dimensions into their work. In this way, even plays that were rarely performed in his lifetime exerted a lasting influence, shaping the ethos of experimental and countercultural creativity for decades to come.


## Crowley's Legacy in Performance and Interpretation

Although *Tannhäuser* and *Household Gods* are rarely staged, the depth of Crowley's symbolism and philosophical insight has continued to inspire directors, performers, and scholars interested in experimental and mystical approaches to theatre. His conception of drama as ritual anticipates modern explorations of immersive, symbolic, or avant-garde theatre.

Crowley's works have served as touchstones for occult theatre and ritualized performance. Directors drawn to mystical or esoteric traditions see in his plays a precedent for integrating symbolism, archetype, and ethical tension into staging. In these interpretations, the theatre becomes more than a venue for entertainment; it becomes a space in which inner life, moral choice, and spiritual aspiration are enacted visibly, allowing audiences to engage with philosophical and psychological questions experientially.

Experimental adaptations of Crowley's plays have also explored the dynamic interplay between desire, will, and consequence. Contemporary directors can reinterpret Tannhäuser's heroic, mythic conflicts or Household Gods' domestic tensions to emphasize ethical ambiguity, the challenges of aligning actions with purpose, or the subtle psychological struggles underlying ordinary life. Even when removed from their original symbolic and Thelemic context, these plays continue to provide rich material for staging human consciousness and moral development on stage.

In this way, Crowley's theatrical legacy persists less in frequency of performance than in the conceptual frameworks and interpretive possibilities his works offer. His plays provide a model for integrating ritual, psychology, and philosophical inquiry into dramatic form, influencing modern theatre practitioners interested in the transformative potential of performance.

## Enduring Cultural Resonance

Aleister Crowley's influence illustrates that a work's cultural and philosophical impact does not necessarily depend on immediate popular success. While his plays—*Tannhäuser* and *Household Gods*—remained largely unperformed in traditional theatre circuits, their ideas, symbols, and philosophical underpinnings seeped into broader creative networks, leaving a subtle but lasting imprint.

In literature and drama, Crowley's synthesis of myth, ritual, and psychological insight inspired writers and playwrights drawn to symbolist and mystical currents. His work demonstrated how allegory and archetype could be harnessed not merely for aesthetic effect, but as a tool for exploring consciousness, ethical choice, and spiritual growth.

In performance, Crowley's vision of theatre as ritual foreshadowed

257

experimental and avant-garde approaches. Directors and performers seeking to merge art and spiritual exploration found in his plays a model for enacting ethical and psychological tension through symbolic action, stagecraft, and immersive storytelling.

Beyond theatre, Crowley's ethos resonated strongly with countercultural movements of the 20th century. Musicians, visual artists, and spiritual seekers drew inspiration from his principles of True Will, personal freedom, and the integration of creativity and ritual. His blending of myth, symbolism, and ethical inquiry offered a framework for experimentation across multiple media, influencing the aesthetics and philosophy of artists who valued mystical depth and transformative engagement.

Though his plays were marginal in conventional theatre, their ideas found new life across creative and spiritual contexts. Crowley's work endures as a touchstone for those interested in the intersection of philosophy, ritual, and artistic expression. This demonstrates that influence can be measured not just by its initial reception, but by how a visionary's ideas spread through culture, inspiring innovation and reflection for generations.

# THE "WICKEDEST MAN" MYTH
# AND LATER REINTERPRETATIONS

Aleister Crowley's reputation as "the wickedest man in the world" originated in the sensationalist newspapers and periodicals of the Edwardian era. Journalists, often eager to sell scandalous stories to a curious public, amplified reports of his unconventional sexual behavior, magical rituals, and flamboyant lifestyle. Crowley himself, never one to avoid controversy, leaned into the persona, understanding that shock and notoriety could draw attention to his philosophical and mystical work. The resulting image—of a deliberately transgressive, morally unbound figure—was both exaggerated and incomplete, focusing on scandal rather than the intellectual and spiritual dimensions of his life.

Yet this myth did not remain static after his death in 1947. In subsequent decades, cultural attitudes shifted, and Crowley's persona was revisited through new lenses. In the mid-20th century, the burgeoning counterculture of the 1960s and 1970s found inspiration in Crowley's emphasis on personal freedom, spiritual experimentation, and self-determination. Musicians, writers, and artists drew selectively from the "wicked man" image, often valuing the symbolism of rebellion more than the literal behaviors it referenced. Figures like Jimmy Page, David Bowie, and others engaged with Crowley's iconography and writings, integrating elements of ritual, mysticism, and transformation into their own creative expression. In this sense, the myth was not merely debunked but repurposed, transformed into a cultural emblem of exploration and transgression aligned with ethical and artistic experimentation.

Academics and historians have also contributed to a more nuanced understanding. Scholars have reexamined his writings, rituals, and plays, situating Crowley in the context of Edwardian literature, European occult traditions, and early modernist philosophy. They emphasize that his "wickedness" was less a matter of malevolence than of deliberate contravention of social norms and rigorous pursuit of his True Will. In this framework, the sensationalist label becomes a cultural shorthand, concealing the ethical, spiritual, and intellectual rigor that informed his life and work.

Today, the "wickedest man" myth continues to circulate in popular culture, yet it coexists with reinterpretations that highlight Crowley's philosophical, literary, and artistic contributions. The paradox of his legacy—both scandalized and venerated—illustrates the enduring fascination of a figure who deliberately blurred the line between performance and life, art and ritual, morality and freedom. Over time, audiences and scholars have moved from shock to curiosity, from caricature to critical engagement, allowing Crowley's multifaceted identity to emerge from the shadows of sensationalism.

## Mid-20th-Century Occult Reinterpretation

Following Aleister Crowley's death in 1947, a concerted effort emerged among his students, followers, and esoteric societies to reframe his legacy. Members of the Ordo Templi Orientis (O.T.O.), students of the A∴A∴, and other occult practitioners emphasized Crowley not merely as a sensational figure but as a philosopher, teacher, and innovator in spiritual practice. They sought to preserve and transmit his teachings on ritual, magick, and Thelema, highlighting the intellectual and ethical rigor underpinning his work.

Key publications played a pivotal role in this reinterpretation. Israel Regardie's *The Golden Dawn* (originally published in 1937 and revised in later editions) presented Crowley's work within the broader context of ceremonial magick, demonstrating continuity with established esoteric traditions and showing practical applications of his methods. Regardie emphasized disciplined practice, ethical responsibility, and the attainment of spiritual insight, countering the narrative of unbridled debauchery. Similarly, John Symonds' biographical writings portrayed Crowley as a complex thinker and writer, situating his personal eccentricities and controversial behavior within the framework of experimental spirituality rather than simple moral failing.

This mid-century reassessment was both corrective and strategic. By highlighting Crowley's intellectual contributions and spiritual philosophy, these interpreters aimed to preserve his teachings for serious students while separating them from the tabloid scandals that had long defined public perception. The "wickedest man" image remained culturally resonant, but within esoteric circles, Crowley's reputation shifted: he became a master of ritual, a theorist of human will, and a model for disciplined self-realization.

This reinterpretation also laid the groundwork for later cultural engagement. By codifying his practices and clarifying his philosophical aims, these writings allowed subsequent generations to approach Crowley's work thoughtfully, encouraging study, adaptation, and creative integration rather than mere sensationalist fascination. In this sense, the mid-20th-century occult revival transformed Crowley from a figure of scandal into a lasting spiritual and intellectual influence.

## Popular Culture and the Counterculture

By the 1960s and 1970s, Aleister Crowley had undergone a dramatic transformation in the public imagination. The sensationalized "wickedest man in the world" image that had once scandalized Edwardian society was now reinterpreted by a new generation of artists, musicians, and writers as a symbol of rebellion, personal freedom, and esoteric insight. Crowley's life and persona were no longer simply shocking; they became emblematic of nonconformity, self-exploration, and creative daring.

In music, figures such as Jimmy Page of Led Zeppelin and filmmaker Kenneth Anger embraced Crowley as both a source of inspiration and a cultural icon. Page famously purchased Crowley's former residence, Boleskine House, and incorporated Crowleyan imagery and themes into his art, while Anger drew on the magician's writings and persona in experimental films, blending ritual, sexuality, and symbolism. Crowley's "wickedness," once condemned, was now read as a challenge to conventional morality and an invitation to explore the hidden dimensions of consciousness.

Writers, poets, and visual artists similarly drew from Crowleyan motifs to enrich their creative work. Themes of ritual, transformation, and the pursuit of True Will became narrative and visual devices, framing characters and scenarios that reflected a mystical or liberated approach to life. Crowley himself was often mythologized: his persona, filled with eccentricity and audacity, served as a larger-than-life archetype of spiritual and artistic independence.

This countercultural reinterpretation effectively flipped the narrative. Traits that had once provoked condemnation—experimentation with consciousness, defiance of social norms, and exploration of sexuality—were reframed as heroic, visionary, or avant-garde. Crowley's example inspired a generation to question authority, to integrate creative practice with personal exploration, and to view the boundaries of morality, art, and spirituality as sites for imaginative engagement. In this way, his "wicked" persona persisted, but its meaning shifted: what had been scandal became emblematic of liberation, experimentation, and transformative possibility.

## Scholarly Reassessment

By the late 20th century, academics began to take a more nuanced view of Aleister Crowley, moving beyond the lurid tales of the "wickedest man" to consider his contributions as a writer, philosopher, and thinker. Scholars in literature, religious studies, and cultural history sought to disentangle the mythologized Crowley from the historical figure, emphasizing the intellectual and artistic rigor that underpinned his work.

Critical reassessment highlighted his literary skill, noting that plays such as *Tannhäuser* and *Household Gods* were not mere curiosities of occultism but deliberate, symbolically rich explorations of morality, will, and consciousness. His poetic and dramatic techniques, use of myth, and integration of mystical frameworks revealed a writer deeply engaged with contemporary literary movements, including Symbolism, Decadence, and early Modernism.

Historians and literary scholars also placed Crowley in context, examining how press sensationalism exaggerated eccentricities while obscuring his serious philosophical and spiritual efforts. This approach clarified that behaviors often cited as evidence of moral depravity—sexual experimentation, ritualized practices, or flamboyant public statements— were largely expressions of personal and spiritual exploration rather than malicious intent.

Finally, academic studies traced Crowley's broader influence. His plays' themes, structure, and symbolic strategies resonated with later literary and theatrical experimentation. Researchers have demonstrated that Crowley's work intersected with larger currents in modernist literature, avant-garde theatre, and occult philosophy, making him a figure of enduring relevance not merely as a sensational personality but as a thinker who anticipated and inspired cultural, literary, and spiritual innovation.

## Crowley as a Symbolic Figure

Aleister Crowley's image has evolved into a canvas onto which successive generations project their own interests, anxieties, and aspirations. To some, he embodies the archetype of the proto-punk icon—the ultimate outsider and challenger of authority. To others, he represents a figure of

263

spiritual inquiry and ethical rigor, a misunderstood teacher whose experiments with ritual and consciousness were ethical rather than malicious. Popular media, films, and music often reference Crowley as a mystical antihero, frequently without precisely understanding his philosophy, and thus they perpetuate the myth in a stylized form.

A notable example of this phenomenon occurred within the rock world. When Randy Rhoads placed a poster of Aleister Crowley in Ozzy Osbourne's dressing room, Osbourne reportedly remarked, "Who the hell is that guy?" Rhoads explained that Crowley was the subject of a song they performed, highlighting how even within the music industry, Crowley's identity was often reduced to a name and a myth, rather than being recognized for his philosophical contributions.

This anecdote underscores a broader cultural tendency to engage with Crowley as a symbol of rebellion, mystery, or the occult while overlooking the depth of his intellectual and spiritual work. Whether embraced as a countercultural icon or invoked as a figure of intrigue, Crowley's persona continues to captivate, often more for the myths surrounding him than for the substance of his teachings.

### Key Takeaways from Reinterpretation

Crowley's posthumous reputation illustrates the enduring power of myth in shaping cultural memory. The "wickedest man" label, initially intended to scandalize, has proven remarkably resilient, yet over time, the narrative surrounding Crowley has become more complex and multifaceted. By looking beyond sensationalist accounts, it becomes clear that his work — philosophical, literary, and ritual — continues to inspire readers, artists, and spiritual seekers long after his death.

This reinterpretation highlights the fluidity of reputation. When traits that once were condemned as immoral or shocking resonate with emerging cultural currents, people often recast them as visionary or liberatory. In Crowley's case, what early 20th-century society saw as transgression, the pursuit of personal will, the exploration of consciousness, and the integration of spiritual practice into daily life,— has been celebrated in countercultural and artistic contexts as emblematic of freedom, experimentation, and transformative potential.

Ultimately, the examination of Crowley's evolving reputation underscores a broader truth about cultural memory: myth can overshadow fact, but it can also serve as a conduit for reengagement with a figure's actual work. In Crowley's case, the myths surrounding him act as a gateway, inviting successive generations to explore the philosophical, literary, and mystical substance that lies beneath the sensationalized surface. His legacy, therefore, is not merely a product of scandal, but a testament to the ways in which provocative ideas and audacious living can leave a lasting impact on art, thought, and culture.

# CROWLEY AND THE MODERN READER

Aleister Crowley's plays remain surprisingly relevant for contemporary readers and theatregoers. At their core, these works explore timeless human tensions: the pull between discipline and distraction, the struggle to assert individuality against social conformity, and the pursuit of spiritual or ethical growth in everyday life. In *Tannhäuser*, Crowley stages these conflicts on a mythic and heroic scale, yet they remain deeply human. The hero's repeated encounters with temptation and failure serve as a mirror to the reader's or audience's own inner challenges, demonstrating how desire and ambition can both illuminate and obscure the path toward self-realization.

Meanwhile, *Household Gods* brings similar themes into the domestic and mundane sphere. By setting moral and spiritual trials within the routines of daily life, Crowley underscores that the pursuit of self-awareness and True Will is not reserved for extraordinary circumstances. The ordinary becomes a stage for insight. In doing so, the play reminds modern readers that ethical reflection and spiritual growth are accessible at any moment, provided one is attentive and intentional. Crowley's fusion of the mythic and the domestic suggests that the challenges of heroism are present in every life, reframed in ways that speak directly to the contemporary experience.

Another layer of relevance lies in Crowley's attention to the tension between individuality and social expectation. Both plays explore how external pressures — tradition, social roles, moral conventions — can conflict with personal desire and authentic purpose. Crowley's characters are frequently confronted with choices that test the alignment of their actions with their inner will. Modern readers, navigating their own cultural, professional, and personal pressures, can recognize themselves in these dilemmas. The plays do not provide simple prescriptions for behavior; rather, they dramatize the complex interplay between selfhood and circumstance, encouraging reflection and critical self-awareness.

Crowley's work also resonates in an era increasingly aware of psychological complexity. Characters are not defined merely by archetypes or plot functions; they are portrayed as morally and spiritually dynamic, struggling with awareness, temptation, and responsibility. This emphasis on interior life allows the plays to speak across a century, offering insight into the universality of human striving. By dramatizing ethical and spiritual growth as a lived experience, Crowley invites modern readers to engage not only with narrative and character but with their own choices and inner development.

In sum, the relevance of Crowley's plays today derives from their layered approach to the human condition. They blend the mythic with the mundane, the symbolic with the concrete, and the ethical with the psychological. They challenge readers to consider how they navigate the tensions of daily life, how they assert individuality while participating in community, and how they cultivate discipline and awareness amidst the distractions and temptations of contemporary existence. By presenting these struggles in both heroic and domestic registers, Crowley ensures that the lessons of his plays are not confined to historical curiosity; they remain living, breathing reflections on the demands and possibilities of human life.

### Reading Crowley as Personal Exploration

Engaging with Aleister Crowley's plays is not merely an exercise in literary analysis; it is an invitation to examine one's own life through the lens of ethical, spiritual, and psychological inquiry. Crowley's central principle — the discovery and enactment of one's True Will — extends naturally from his philosophy into his dramatic works. Unlike conventional didactic texts, his plays do not dictate right or wrong; they dramatize the consequences of choice and the ongoing effort required for self-mastery. This approach transforms reading or viewing into an active process, encouraging reflection, introspection, and personal engagement.

In both *Tannhäuser* and *Household Gods*, characters are presented as mirrors of the audience's own struggles. The mythic hero faces trials that dramatize the alignment of desire with purpose, showing that spiritual and moral growth demands attention, courage, and perseverance. Conversely, the domestic setting of *Household Gods* demonstrates that self-awareness and ethical reflection are equally necessary in everyday life. Crowley's skill lies in connecting these two scales, the heroic and the ordinary, allowing the reader to see that the pursuit of True Will is continuous, manifest in both monumental and mundane choices.

This emphasis on lived experience makes the plays uniquely suited for modern readers. They illustrate that personal exploration is not abstract or removed from the world; it is enacted moment by moment. The plays provide concrete examples of characters wrestling with temptation, ambition, and duty, yet always in ways that resonate with contemporary concerns. Readers can observe the consequences of inaction as clearly as the rewards of alignment with inner purpose, offering a nuanced model for reflection.

Crowley also invites readers to participate in the drama of consciousness itself. Characters' inner lives are portrayed with a combination of symbolic imagery, dialogue, and narrative structure that externalizes ethical and spiritual struggle. Mirrors, thresholds, roads, and mountains become stages for the inner journey, creating opportunities for the audience to connect symbol with personal meaning. By following these arcs, the reader is encouraged to consider their own patterns of desire, resistance, and growth. In effect, the plays function as a form of guided introspection, blending storytelling with philosophical and spiritual exercise.

Importantly, Crowley's work fosters exploration rather than dogma. His plays do not prescribe rigid rules; they demonstrate processes, tensions, and outcomes. This openness allows readers to engage creatively, drawing insights relevant to their own circumstances, beliefs, and aspirations. The invitation is to witness, reflect, and integrate — to observe how ethical decision-making, attention to will, and the balance between inner aspiration and outer reality operate in one's own life.

Ultimately, reading Crowley as a tool for personal exploration aligns with the broader aim of his philosophy. The stage, the narrative, and the symbolic framework all converge to encourage self-awareness, deliberate action, and the cultivation of moral and spiritual discernment. By participating mentally and emotionally in the drama, modern readers gain more than literary appreciation; they are invited into an active process of self-examination, echoing the transformative goals of Crowley's magick, not as ritual alone but as an awakening of consciousness and responsibility.

## The Enduring Significance of Crowley's Art

Aleister Crowley's plays continue to resonate because they engage with universal questions of consciousness, choice, and transformation. Their significance lies not merely in historical or occult interest, but in their capacity to illuminate human experience across time and culture. By blending narrative, symbolism, and ethical reflection, Crowley crafted works that invite audiences and readers to confront the perennial tension between aspiration and habit, self-knowledge and distraction, individuality and societal expectation.

One of the most striking aspects of his plays is their dual scope. In *Tannhäuser*, Crowley dramatizes the heroic journey in mythic terms. The grandeur of the narrative amplifies the stakes, showing how alignment with one's True Will is both a personal and a cosmic endeavor. In *Household Gods*, the same principles are embedded in domestic, everyday situations, demonstrating that spiritual and ethical challenges are not confined to legend or ritual but are present in ordinary life. This duality reinforces the enduring relevance of his work: the lessons it imparts are applicable whether one is facing extraordinary or routine circumstances.

Crowley's artistry also lies in his use of symbolic and ritualized language. The imagery of mirrors, thresholds, mountains, and roads externalizes internal processes, allowing readers and viewers to witness the interplay between desire, discipline, and moral responsibility. Through these symbols, the abstract becomes tangible, offering a pathway to reflection and insight that is accessible without prior esoteric training. This symbolic universality helps his plays speak to audiences across generations, bridging literary, spiritual, and cultural contexts.

Another source of lasting significance is Crowley's treatment of choice and consequence. Unlike traditional morality plays, his works do not impose ethical judgment from an external authority. Instead, they dramatize the process of self-determination, showing that ethical awareness and spiritual growth emerge from conscious engagement with life. Readers are encouraged to see themselves in the characters' struggles, recognizing that self-mastery and insight require attention, courage, and deliberate action. The plays thus function as both mirror and guide, making the pursuit of personal and spiritual development an immediate and lived experience.

Crowley's fusion of art and magick also contributes to their contemporary relevance. His conception of theatre as ritual — the performance of transformation — anticipates modern explorations of interactive and immersive performance, as well as practices that blend creativity with personal development. Even absent formal staging, the texts carry an energy of enactment: the reader or viewer becomes an active participant in the moral and spiritual dynamics of the narrative. This makes the work not simply something to be observed, but something to be experienced and integrated.

Finally, the endurance of Crowley's art is amplified by its openness. His plays do not demand adherence to a specific philosophy or belief system. Instead, they offer frameworks for inquiry, reflection, and imagination, allowing each reader or performer to engage with the work according to their own context and curiosity. In this sense, Crowley's magick is not confined to ritual or ceremonial practice; it resides in the capacity of his art to awaken consciousness, foster ethical awareness, and inspire creative engagement with life itself.

In sum, the enduring significance of Crowley's plays lies in their ability to illuminate the human journey in ways both symbolic and practical, mythic and mundane. They invite reflection on personal will, moral responsibility, and the pursuit of insight, bridging literature, philosophy, and spirituality. For the modern reader, these works are as much a guide to self-awareness and ethical discernment as they are examples of experimental drama, proving that Crowley's art, far from being merely scandalous or eccentric, continues to speak to fundamental aspects of human existence.

## Why Crowley Still Matters

Aleister Crowley's plays endure not simply as artifacts of a particular historical moment, but as living works that challenge readers and audiences to engage deeply with the questions of self, choice, and transformation. At their core, his dramas explore the tension between distraction and discipline, conformity and individuality, and the spiritual possibilities inherent in everyday life. Whether in the heroic, mythic landscape of *Tannhäuser* or the domestic, satirical world of *Household Gods*, Crowley illustrates that moral and ethical development, as well as spiritual insight, are cultivated through attentive engagement with the world around us.

Reading Crowley today invites a different experience than it might have in his own time. The scandal, the mythology, and the sensationalist image of the "wickedest man in the world" have largely faded, leaving space for thoughtful reflection. The modern reader can approach his work not with moral judgment, but with curiosity, and explore how it illuminates the inner life, human aspiration, and the pursuit of True Will. Crowley's dramas encourage self-examination: by witnessing the struggles of his characters. Audiences are invited to consider the forces shaping their own decisions, the patterns of desire and habit, and the ways in which ethical and spiritual growth is possible in ordinary circumstances.

Crowley's genius lies in the fusion of art and magick. His plays are not only texts to read, but experiences to inhabit. The theatre becomes a space for reflection, a mirror for the human spirit, and a laboratory for ethical and spiritual inquiry. In this sense, the transformative potential of his work extends beyond staged performance; it manifests in the attentive, engaged reader or viewer who considers the drama of inner life as seriously as the drama enacted on the stage.

Ultimately, Aleister Crowley's art matters because it awakens self-awareness. His symbols, narratives, and philosophical frameworks invite personal exploration, offering insights into the dynamics of desire, will, and moral responsibility. The "magick" of Crowley's plays is not found solely in ceremonial ritual, but in the capacity of literature and theatre to illuminate the human journey, to inspire reflection, and to encourage deliberate, conscious living.

For the modern reader, then, engaging with Crowley is an exercise in discovery: of self, of ethical principle, and of the potential for transformation in both extraordinary and mundane life. His work reminds us that the pursuit of understanding and the cultivation of insight are not the province of the past, the mystical, or the heroic alone — they are woven into the fabric of every conscious choice, every moment of reflection, and every encounter with the symbolic and the real. In this way, Crowley's plays remain both relevant and profoundly instructive, offering pathways to self-knowledge, moral discernment, and the awakening of higher consciousness.

# DISCUSSION QUESTIONS

## For Tannhäuser

1. How does Crowley's version invert Wagner's original narrative, and what does that inversion reveal about his views on redemption and spiritual authority?

2. What is the metaphysical significance of Venus in this play? Is she merely a temptress, or does she represent a deeper spiritual force?

3. How does Crowley use ritual and invocation within the dramatic structure—are these theatrical devices or genuine magical operations?

4. What does the play suggest about the tension between sensual experience and spiritual aspiration? Is either path resolved or transcended?

5. How is the Grail reinterpreted in Crowley's version, and what does that say about his relationship to Christian symbolism?

6. In what ways does the play reflect Thelemic principles, especially the concept of True Will?

7. How does the use of poetic and ritual language function as a vehicle for esoteric meaning?

8. Is Tannhäuser a seeker, a rebel, or a pawn? How does his journey reflect Crowley's own spiritual conflicts?

9. How do the ecclesiastical figures and pilgrims function symbolically rather than psychologically?

10. If you were staging Tannhäuser today, would you emphasize its ritual elements or strip them back? Why?

11. Which character would be most difficult to portray authentically —and what would that performance require?

12. What modern setting could serve as a backdrop for a contemporary adaptation without losing the play's metaphysical core?

## For Household Gods

1. • Is Household Gods truly a comedy, or is the humor a mask for deeper metaphysical critique?

2. • How does Crowley use satire to challenge domestic norms, religious authority, and cultural conformity?

3. • What does the protagonist's transformation suggest about spiritual awakening in mundane settings?

4. • Are the "gods" literal, metaphorical, or psychological? How does their presence reshape the domestic space?

5. • How does the play engage with Thelemic ideas of liberation, autonomy, and magical consciousness?

6. • What role does inversion play in the structure of the play—ritual, gender, authority?

7. • Which character most clearly embodies Crowley's philosophical stance—and which resists it?

8. • How does the protagonist's arc compare to Tannhäuser's? Are they both seeking the same kind of truth?

9. • If you could insert one modern appliance or technology into the household, what would it be—and how would the gods react?

10. • Which scene would benefit most from being staged as absurdist theatre?

11. What would a sequel look like? Would the protagonist relapse into conformity or evolve further?

# SUGGESTED READING AND VIEWING

## Selected Bibliography of Aleister Crowley

### Magick and Philosophy

- *The Book of the Law (Liber AL vel Legis)*

Written in Cairo in April 1904, Crowley claimed the book was dictated to him by a non-human intelligence named Aiwass, whom he described as a messenger of the gods. The text is divided into three chapters, each delivered by a different deity from the Thelemic pantheon:

Chapter I: Nuit — The goddess of infinite space and possibility. Her voice celebrates love, freedom, and the boundless nature of existence. She invites humanity to embrace joy and expansion.

Chapter II: Hadit — The point of consciousness and individual will. Hadit speaks of the power within each person, urging the reader to seek their True Will—the unique path of purpose and fulfillment.

Chapter III: Ra-Hoor-Khuit — The god of war and vengeance, representing the active force of the new Aeon. His tone is more militant, calling for strength, discipline, and the overthrow of outdated moral systems.

The book is written in poetic, cryptic language, filled with mystical symbolism, numerology, and esoteric references. It challenges conventional morality and religious dogma, offering instead a vision of spiritual sovereignty and cosmic alignment.

*The Book of the Law* established Crowley's spiritual system, Thelema, which centers on the pursuit of one's True Will—a concept blending destiny, purpose, and divine alignment. Crowley declared the arrival of the Aeon of Horus, a new spiritual age marked by self-realization, freedom, and the rejection of authoritarian religious structures. The book became the cornerstone of modern ceremonial magick, influencing generations of occultists, artists, and spiritual seekers. Its provocative language—especially the famous dictum "Do what thou wilt"—has been misunderstood as promoting selfishness or lawlessness, though Crowley insisted it referred to one's divine purpose, not whim.

This text is essential for understanding Crowley's worldview and the spiritual context behind his dramatic works.

- *777 and Other Qabalistic Writings* (1909)

*777 and Other Qabalistic Writings* of Aleister Crowley is a foundational text for understanding the symbolic and numerical framework behind Crowley's magickal system. It is a reference manual of correspondences—bridging astrology, tarot, alchemy, and mysticism—that reveals the hidden architecture of ritual and spiritual practice.

Originally published in 1909, *777* is a compilation of three key texts:

1. *Liber 777* — A massive table of correspondences linking Hebrew letters, tarot cards, astrological signs, magical weapons, deities, colors, scents, and more across dozens of spiritual systems. It is designed to help magicians construct rituals with symbolic precision.

2. *Sepher Sephiroth* — A dictionary of Hebrew words and their numerical values (gematria), used to uncover hidden meanings and connections between concepts.

3. *An Essay on the Qabalah* — Crowley's introduction to the philo-

sophical and mystical significance of the Qabalah, explaining how numbers and symbols reflect spiritual truths.

The book is not narrative—it is a toolkit. Crowley believed that understanding symbolic relationships was essential to effective magick. *777* offers a way to decode those relationships and build rituals that resonate across multiple traditions.

*777 and Other Qabalistic Writings* serves as the symbolic backbone of Thelemic magick. Crowley used these correspondences to design rituals, interpret visions, and align spiritual forces. The tables link Jewish mysticism with Egyptian, Greek, Hindu, and Christian systems, reflecting Crowley's universal approach. Magicians use *777* to select ritual elements, interpret dreams, and explore the deeper meaning of spiritual experiences. It became a standard reference for the Hermetic Order of the Golden Dawn, the A∴A∴, and the Ordo Templi Orientis.

If *Magick in Theory and Practice* is the "how," *777* is the "what"—the raw symbolic material that magicians shape into ritual.

- ### *The Vision and the Voice (Liber 418)* (1911)

*The Vision and the Voice (Liber 418)* is Aleister Crowley's mystical record of visionary experiences received in the Algerian desert in 1909. It is one of his most profound spiritual texts, chronicling encounters with angelic intelligences and revealing the metaphysical structure of the universe through the Enochian system of magick.

Crowley undertook a series of magical workings with his associate Victor Neuburg, using the Enochian Calls—a system of angelic invocations developed by John Dee and Edward Kelley in the 16th century. Each call opened a gateway to one of the 30 Aethyrs, or spiritual realms, which Crowley explored in trance-like states.

The book documents:

- Visions of cosmic archetypes: Crowley encounters gods, angels, and symbolic figures representing spiritual truths.
- Revelations about the soul and initiation: Each Aethyr presents

challenges, insights, and transformations, mirroring the path of spiritual ascent.

• Thelemic prophecy: The visions reinforce and expand the doctrines of *The Book of the Law*, including the nature of True Will and the Aeon of Horus.

• Personal transformation: Crowley's own spiritual evolution unfolds through the text, culminating in mystical union and insight.

The writing blends poetic imagery, esoteric symbolism, and raw emotional intensity. It is not a manual—it is a spiritual diary, revealing the inner landscape of a magician confronting the divine.

*The Vision and the Voice* deepens Thelemic doctrine by clarifying and expanding ideas introduced in *The Book of the Law*. Crowley's work reestablished the Enochian system as central to modern ceremonial magick. It stands as one of his most intimate and transformative texts, showing mystical vulnerability and ambition. The A∴A∴ and other groups use it as a guide for advanced spiritual work.

This book is essential for understanding the mystical and symbolic depth behind Crowley's dramatic works. Where Tannhäuser and *Household Gods* dramatize spiritual struggle, *The Vision and the Voice* reveals the inner terrain of that struggle in vivid, transcendent detail.

• *Magick in Theory and Practice* (1929)

*Magick in Theory and Practice* is Aleister Crowley's definitive manual on ceremonial magick, offering both philosophical foundations and detailed instructions for ritual work. It is essential reading for understanding Crowley's spiritual system and the practical application of Thelema.

Originally published in 1929 as *Part III of Book Four (Liber ABA)*, this work is Crowley's most comprehensive guide to the theory and execution of magick. He famously defines magick as:

The book is divided into sections that explore:

• The nature of magick: Crowley explains magick as a disciplined spiritual practice, not superstition or fantasy. It is about aligning one's actions with one's True Will.

• The role of the magician: The practitioner is seen as a spiritual scientist, using ritual, symbolism, and concentration to transform consciousness.

• Tools and rituals: Detailed descriptions of ceremonial implements (wand, cup, sword, pentacle), invocations, and symbolic gestures.

• Initiation and progress: Crowley outlines stages of spiritual development, including purification, invocation, and union with the divine.

The tone is both scholarly and mystical, blending classical references, occult symbolism, and personal insight. Crowley draws from Hermeticism, Kabbalah, yoga, and Eastern philosophy to build a universal framework for spiritual transformation.

*Magick in Theory and Practice* serves as a practical cornerstone of Thelema. While *The Book of the Law* lays out the philosophy, this work shows how to live it. It shaped the practices of the Ordo Templi Orientis (O.T.O.) and influenced generations of magicians, artists, and spiritual seekers. Crowley integrates Eastern techniques (such as pranayama and dharana) with Western ritual, making it one of the earliest cross-cultural spiritual manuals. Despite its depth, Crowley intended the book to guide newcomers into magickal practice with clarity and rigor.

This book is crucial for understanding the spiritual and philosophical context behind Crowley's dramatic works. Where *Tannhäuser* and *Household Gods* explore mystical themes through art, *Magick in Theory and Practice* reveals the mechanics behind that mysticism.

• *Little Essays Toward Truth* (1938)

*Little Essays Toward Truth* is a collection of sixteen philosophical meditations by Aleister Crowley, exploring core spiritual and psychological concepts through the lens of Thelema and Qabalah. It is one of his most mature and introspective works, aimed at readers seeking clarity without ritual or dogma.

Published in 1938, the book presents short essays on fundamental aspects of human experience and spiritual inquiry. Each essay focuses on a single concept:

Man
Trance
Memory
Energy
Sorrow
Knowledge
Wonder
Understanding
Beatitude
Chastity
Laughter
Silence
Indifference
Love
Mastery
Truth

Crowley approaches each topic with a blend of mystical insight, psychological depth, and philosophical rigor. He draws heavily on Qabalistic symbolism, Thelemic doctrine, and classical philosophy, but writes in a style that is more reflective and personal than his ritual texts.

The essays are not instructional—they are exploratory, inviting contemplation of the nature of reality, consciousness, and spiritual growth. Crowley often challenges conventional morality and encourages the pursuit of truth through direct experience and disciplined thought.

*Little Essays Toward Truth* offers philosophical clarity through lucid reflections accessible to thoughtful readers. It distills Crowley's mystical worldview into concise, meditative essays. While *Magick in Theory and Practice* teaches how to perform magick, this work explores why one might pursue it. The topics—love, sorrow, mastery, truth—remain central to spiritual inquiry across traditions.

This book presents Crowley not only as a dramatist or magician, but as a philosopher engaged with the human condition. It stands as a quiet, powerful counterpoint to the theatrical intensity of *Tannhäuser* and *Household Gods*.

- *Eight Lectures on Yoga* (1939)

*Eight Lectures on Yoga* is Aleister Crowley's most accessible and practical guide to yogic philosophy and practice, blending Eastern tradition with Western occult insight. It demystifies yoga for beginners while offering deep metaphysical reflections for advanced students.

Originally delivered as a series of talks in 1937 and published in 1939, the book is divided into two parts:

Part I: "Yoga for Yahoos"

Crowley introduces yoga in plain, often humorous language, aiming to strip away exoticism and superstition. He explains:

- What yoga is not (e.g., mere stretching or mysticism)
- The eight limbs of yoga (from Patanjali's Yoga Sutras): yama, niyama, asana, pranayama, pratyahara, dharana, dhyana, and samadhi
- The purpose of yoga: to still the mind and unite the self with the divine

He emphasizes discipline, skepticism, and direct experience, mocking both blind faith and shallow spiritualism.

Part II: "Yoga for Yellowbellies"

This section dives deeper into the philosophical and mystical implications of yoga:

- The nature of consciousness and illusion
- The role of the ego and the process of transcendence
- The parallels between yoga and ceremonial magick

Crowley draws connections between Eastern and Western systems, showing how yoga complements Thelemic practice.

*Eight Lectures on Yoga* is one of Crowley's clearest and most humorous works, ideal for newcomers to yoga or magick. It integrates Hindu philosophy with Western esotericism, showing their shared goals. The book offers both step-by-step guidance and deep metaphysical insight, and helped establish yoga as a core component of Thelemic and Western spiritual practice.

Where *The Vision and the Voice* presents Crowley's mystical heights, *Eight Lectures on Yoga* reveals his grounded, methodical side.


• *Magick Without Tears* (1947)

Written during the 1940s and published posthumously in 1954, this book compiles Aleister Crowley's correspondence with a female student who asked for plainspoken explanations of his teachings. The result is a series of essays that cover:

• The nature of magick: Crowley defines magick as the art of aligning action with True Will and explains how it differs from superstition or fantasy.

• Thelemic principles: He clarifies key ideas from The Book of the Law, including the Aeon of Horus, the concept of True Will, and the rejection of conventional morality.

• Practical advice: Topics include ritual structure, meditation, astral travel, initiation, and the use of magical tools.

• Philosophical depth: Crowley discusses ethics, reincarnation, the soul, and the role of the magician in society.

The tone is informal, witty, and often sarcastic. Crowley is clearly enjoying the chance to teach without the constraints of ritual or symbolism.

*Magick Without Tears* is one of Crowley's most readable works, ideal for beginners who find his other texts too dense or cryptic. It revisits ideas from *Magick in Theory and Practice*, *The Book of the Law*, and *777*, explaining them in everyday language. The letter format reveals Crowley's personality —his humor, impatience, brilliance, and warmth. Many occultists use this book as a day-to-day guide for living Thelemically and practicing magick.

This was Crowley's final major work, written during the last years of his life. It stands as a summation of his teachings, offering clarity, accessibility, and personal insight at the close of his career.


## Poetry and Literature


- *White Stains* (1898)

Published in Amsterdam by Leonard Smithers, *White Stains* was Aleister Crowley's attempt to rewrite Richard von Krafft-Ebing's *Psychopathia Sexualis* in lyrical form. The poems are written in both English and French and include:

- Explicit sexual themes: Many poems celebrate homosexuality, masturbation, and other taboo subjects, often with graphic intensity.
- Mystical and symbolic undertones: Despite its eroticism, the work is steeped in Crowley's emerging occult worldview, linking desire with transcendence.
- Decadent literary style: Influenced by fin-de-siècle writers like Baudelaire and Swinburne, Crowley uses lush imagery and classical references to elevate the material beyond mere shock value.

The collection includes pieces such as *A Ballad of Passive Paederasty*, *Ode to Venus Callipyge*, and *Volupté*, each pushing the boundaries of Victorian morality.

*White Stains* marks an early expression of Crowley's radicalism, signaling his break from conventional morality and his embrace of spiritual and sexual liberation. It aligns him with the Decadent movement, challenging censorship and societal norms. The poems hint at later Thelemic ideas, where sexuality becomes a path to mystical insight. The book was considered obscene and suppressed for decades; its underground reputation contributed to Crowley's mythos as a transgressive figure.

This work positions Crowley not only as a playwright or magician, but as a literary provocateur who used poetry to explore the shadow side of human nature and spiritual ecstasy.

- *The Sword of Song* (1904)

*The Sword of Song* is Aleister Crowley's 1904 satirical and philosophical poetry collection, blending biting wit with deep metaphysical inquiry. It marks one of his earliest public declarations of Thelemic ideas and his rejection of conventional religion.

Subtitled *Called by Christians The Book of the Beast*, this work is composed of two long poems—"*Ascension Day*" and "*Pentecoste*"—alongside extensive footnotes and essays. Crowley uses these pieces to:

- Critique Christianity: He mocks religious dogma, biblical literalism, and moral hypocrisy.
- Explore Buddhism and agnosticism: Crowley reflects on his own spiritual journey, including his time studying Buddhism and his embrace of skepticism.
- Introduce Thelemic themes: Though not yet fully formed, ideas like True Will, spiritual liberation, and the rejection of guilt begin to surface.
- Declare his identity as "The Beast": Crowley embraces the title given to him by critics, turning it into a badge of spiritual rebellion.

The poems are dense with literary and philosophical references, and the footnotes often rival the verse in length and complexity. Crowley's style is deliberately provocative, mixing humor, blasphemy, and mystical insight.

*The Sword of Song* stands as one of Crowley's first works to articulate the ideas that would later define Thelema. The fusion of poetry, satire, and scholarly annotation showcases his unique approach to spiritual literature. The book engages with Nietzsche, Kant, and Buddhist thought, revealing Crowley's intellectual range. Its content was considered too blasphemous and controversial for English publishers, so Crowley printed it privately in Paris in a limited run of approximately 100 copies. The refusal by publishers to handle the book underscored Crowley's outsider status and his commitment to challenging religious and cultural norms.

This work positions Crowley as a literary rebel and philosophical provocateur—qualities that echo through Tannhäuser and *Household Gods*. It serves as a bridge between his poetic beginnings and his later magickal system.

### *Clouds Without Water* (1909)

The book is framed as a hoax: Crowley pretends to be a Christian minister who has discovered and annotated a scandalous manuscript of decadent poetry. The "editor" condemns the poems in footnotes, while the actual content celebrates mystical and erotic experience.

Key features include:

• Poems of spiritual longing and sensual ecstasy, often blending Christian imagery with pagan and occult themes.

• Satirical commentary from the fake editor, who denounces the poems with moral outrage—ironically highlighting their beauty and insight.

• Themes of hypocrisy and repression, especially in religious institutions that deny the sacredness of desire.

The title comes from the Bible (Jude 1:12), referring to false prophets —"clouds without water"—who promise spiritual nourishment but deliver emptiness. Crowley flips this metaphor, suggesting that institutional religion is the real deception, while mystical experience offers true fulfillment.

*Clouds Without Water* is a masterclass in irony, using satire to critique religious dogma and elevate mystical sensuality. The poems reflect Crowley's evolving Thelemic philosophy, where love and will are sacred forces. It aligns him with the Decadent movement and shares thematic ground with earlier works like *White Stains* and later ones such as *Moonchild*. Due to its format and content, the book was considered too controversial for general publication and was privately printed in London in 1909 under the pseudonym "Rev. C. Verey." It was circulated only among ministers of religion, and its rarity contributed to its cult status among occultists and literary rebels.

This work presents Crowley as a literary trickster—someone who used poetry not just to express mystical truths, but to challenge the moral and spiritual status quo.

- *The Diary of a Drug Fiend* (1922)

This is Aleister Crowley's first published novel, and it's a gripping, semi-autobiographical tale of addiction, despair, and spiritual redemption. Written in the aftermath of World War I, it follows two lovers—Sir Peter Pendragon and Lou Laleham—as they spiral into drug addiction and attempt to reclaim their lives through magick and Thelemic philosophy.

The story unfolds in three parts:

1. Paradiso – Peter and Lou fall in love and begin experimenting with cocaine and heroin, believing they've found ecstasy and freedom.

2. Inferno – Addiction takes hold. Their lives unravel as they descend into paranoia, poverty, and emotional devastation.

3. Purgatorio – With the help of the magician King Lamus (a stand-in for Crowley), they begin the painful process of recovery through spiritual discipline and the discovery of their True Will.

Crowley uses the novel to dramatize his belief that magick and Thelema offer a path out of addiction and despair, not through repression, but through alignment with one's divine purpose.

*Diary of a Drug Fiend* is the first novel to explore Thelema in action— how spiritual principles can transform real lives. Crowley draws from personal experience, making this one of the earliest literary treatments of drug addiction as a spiritual crisis. The book presents ceremonial magick not as fantasy, but as a therapeutic and transformative practice. It remains culturally relevant and is still cited in discussions of occultism, addiction literature, and spiritual psychology. First published in 1922 by Collins in London, it marked a bold literary debut and a public declaration of Crowley's belief in the redemptive power of the True Will.

This work presents Crowley as a novelist who used fiction to tackle real-world suffering—and offer mystical solutions.

- *Moonchild* (1929)

*Moonchild* is Aleister Crowley's most famous novel, blending occult warfare, romantic tragedy, and mystical allegory. Written in 1917, it dramatizes a magical battle between two rival groups of magicians vying for control over a woman destined to give birth to a spiritually evolved child —the Moonchild.

The story follows Lisa la Giuffria, a young woman caught between two occult factions:

- The White Lodge, led by the magician Simon Iff (a fictionalized version of Crowley), seeks to guide Lisa through a series of magical rituals to conceive the Moonchild—a being of pure will and spiritual power.

- The Black Lodge, composed of sinister and manipulative magicians, aims to corrupt or destroy the process.

As Lisa undergoes initiation and transformation, the novel explores:

- Magical theory and ritual: Crowley embeds real ceremonial practices and Thelemic philosophy throughout the narrative.

- Psychological and spiritual development: Lisa's journey reflects the trials of the soul seeking enlightenment.

- Satire and symbolism: Crowley mocks spiritual pretenders, Victorian morality, and even his own peers in the occult world.

The tone shifts between mystical seriousness and biting satire, with vivid descriptions of astral travel, magical combat, and spiritual ecstasy.

*Moonchild* is one of the earliest novels to incorporate real magical systems into its plot. The Moonchild represents the birth of a new spiritual consciousness aligned with Crowley's vision of the Aeon of Horus. Simon Iff, a recurring figure in Crowley's fiction, embodies the wise, ironic magician archetype. The novel inspired later occult writers and remains a touchstone for esoteric literature. Though written in 1917, it was not published until 1929 by the Mandrake Press, due to its controversial content and the difficulty of securing a publisher.

This work presents Crowley as a storyteller who used fiction to dramatize his spiritual ideals. It is a vivid, strange, and often beautiful expression of Thelemic magick in narrative form.

- *Orpheus: A Lyrical Legend* (1929)

The poem reimagines the myth of Orpheus, the legendary musician who descends into the underworld to retrieve his beloved Eurydice. But Crowley's version is far from a simple retelling—it is a sprawling, esoteric journey through:

- The soul's descent and return: Orpheus becomes a symbol of the initiate, descending into darkness to reclaim divine truth.
- Mystical allegory: The poem is layered with Qabalistic, Thelemic, and Hermetic symbolism, reflecting Crowley's evolving spiritual system.
- Musical structure: Divided into acts and cantos, the poem mimics operatic form, with recurring motifs and tonal shifts.
- Philosophical inquiry: Themes of illusion, suffering, ecstasy, and transcendence are explored through dense, lyrical language.

Crowley considered *Orpheus* a major artistic achievement, though it was largely ignored or misunderstood in his lifetime due to its difficulty and esoteric content. It was privately printed in 1905 by the Society for the Propagation of Religious Truth at Boleskine, his estate in Inverness. The limited distribution and dense symbolism contributed to its obscurity.

*Orpheus: A Lyrical Legend* is one of Crowley's longest and most structurally complex works, showcasing his poetic skill and intellectual range. Orpheus's journey mirrors Crowley's own path as a seeker, magician, and prophet. The poem fuses classical narrative with occult philosophy, making it a key text for understanding Crowley's symbolic universe. Though less famous than his ritual texts, *Orpheus* is central to appreciating Crowley as a serious literary figure—not just a mystic or provocateur.

This work positions Crowley as a mythmaker and poet of real depth—someone who used art not just to shock, but to illuminate the soul's journey through darkness and light.

- *The Confessions of Aleister Crowley* (1929–1930)

Crowley began writing this massive autobiography in the 1920s, intending it to span six volumes. Only two were published during his lifetime, under the title The Spirit of Solitude, and later reissued as The Confessions of Aleister Crowley. The subtitle "An Autohagiography" reflects his ironic self-image as both saint and sinner.

The book covers:

- His childhood and education: Including his strict Plymouth Brethren upbringing and rebellion against it.
- Mountaineering exploits: Adventures in the Alps and Himalayas, showcasing his physical daring.
- Magical initiation: His involvement with the Hermetic Order of the Golden Dawn and founding of the A∴A∴.
- Travel and mysticism: Journeys through India, China, and Egypt, where he received The Book of the Law.
- Literary and artistic life: His poetry, plays, and controversial public persona.
- Sexual and spiritual philosophy: Reflections on Thelema, magick, and the role of sexuality in spiritual awakening.

Crowley writes with flamboyance, wit, and unapologetic ego, blending factual detail with mythic self-portraiture.

*The Confessions of Aleister Crowley* is the most detailed account of Crowley's life in his own words. It offers firsthand explanations of Thelemic doctrine and magical practice. The book also chronicles the occult revival of the early 20th century and Crowley's role in it. Combining memoir, travelogue, and philosophical essay, it stands as a unique literary artifact. The first two volumes were published between 1929 and 1930 by the Mandrake Press, but the full six-volume project was never completed. The existing text ends before Crowley's final years, which are covered in other biographies.

This work remains the central autobiographical source for understanding Crowley's life, thought, and mythic self-construction.

- *Olla: An Anthology of Sixty Years of Song* (1946)

Published near the end of Crowley's life, *Olla* is a curated selection of poems spanning six decades. The title, Latin for "pot" or "stew," reflects the eclectic nature of the collection—a mix of styles, themes, and moods.

The anthology includes:
- Early romantic and decadent verse from the 1890s, showing Crowley's literary roots in the fin-de-siècle tradition.
- Mystical and Thelemic poetry that emerged as his spiritual philosophy matured.
- Erotic and satirical pieces, often provocative and irreverent.
- Philosophical and reflective works, revealing his inner struggles, insights, and aspirations.

Crowley arranged the poems to reflect his personal and spiritual journey, making *Olla* not just a literary collection but a kind of poetic autobiography.

*Olla* preserves Crowley's poetic voice for posterity, highlighting his range and depth. The poems offer glimpses into his mystical experiences and Thelemic worldview. Crowley's refusal to conform—sexually, spiritually, artistically—is evident throughout. As one of his final works, *Olla* was published in 1946 by the Ordo Templi Orientis in London in a limited edition of 500 copies, with a special run of 20 copies printed on pre-war mould-made paper. It stands as a capstone to his literary career and a valuable resource for scholars and seekers alike.

This collection gives readers a sense of Crowley's full poetic arc—from youthful rebellion to mystical maturity. It complements his dramatic works, showing how poetry remained a constant thread in his spiritual and artistic life.

- *The Equinox* (1909–1937)

*The Equinox* was Aleister Crowley's official journal of the A∴A∴, subtitled The Review of Scientific Illuminism. It was designed to present occult knowledge with the structure and seriousness of academic publishing. Crowley used it to disseminate rituals, essays, poetry, fiction, and ceremonial texts, establishing a public record of his evolving spiritual system. The journal became the central publishing vehicle for Thelemic doctrine and remains one of the most important sources for understanding Crowley's work.

Volume I (1909–1913)

Ten issues, labeled *Vol. I, Nos. I–X*, published semi-annually. This volume includes foundational A∴A∴ texts, rituals, essays, poetry, and fiction. Key contents include Liber O, Liber E, The Rites of Eleusis, *The Temple of Solomon the King*, and *The Book of the Law*.

Volume II

Planned but never published. Some material intended for this volume was later absorbed into Volume III or issued independently.

Volume III (1919–1944)

Four known issues:

- No. I (*The Blue Equinox*, 1919): Introduces the O.T.O., includes *Liber II, Liber XV (Gnostic Mass)*, and *Liber Samekh*.
- No. II (*The Equinox of the Gods*, 1930s): Focuses on the reception of *The Book of the Law*.
- No. III (*The Heart of the Master*, 1938).
- No. IV (*Shih Yi: A Critical and Mnemonic Paraphrase of the Yi King*, 1944).

Volume II was abandoned due to shifting priorities and the post-WWI publishing climate. Crowley moved on to other projects, and the scale of the journal became unsustainable. Some scholars speculate that Liber Aleph or The Book of Lies might have been candidates for inclusion, but they were published independently.

**Note:**

Aleister Crowley's literary and magical output was vast, spanning poetry, fiction, ritual texts, essays, and philosophical treatises. This selected bibliography highlights works most relevant to the themes explored in *Tannhäuser* and *Household Gods*. Readers interested in exploring further will find that Crowley's later writings expand upon the spiritual, psychological, and artistic ideas introduced in these plays. His life and philosophy are deeply embedded in his creative work, offering insight into the man behind the myth—and into his enduring influence on art, music, theatre, and even religion, including modern Christianity (though many are loath to admit it).

# Secondary Sources on Aleister Crowley

## Biographies and Life Studies

- Richard Kaczynski – *Perdurabo: The Life of Aleister Crowley*

The definitive biography of Crowley, meticulously researched and chronologically structured. Kaczynski presents Crowley not as a caricature, but as a complex figure—mystic, poet, provocateur—whose life and work are inseparable. Essential reading for anyone seeking to understand how Crowley's plays *(Tannhäuser, Household Gods)* fit into his broader spiritual and philosophical evolution.

This biography provides essential context for understanding Crowley's psychological, spiritual, and artistic development. Readers of *Tannhäuser* and *Household Gods* will find direct parallels between the themes in these plays—spiritual conflict, divine immanence, rejection of bourgeois morality—and the events and philosophies that shaped Crowley's life. Kaczynski's work is indispensable for situating the plays within Crowley's broader system and tracing their influence forward.

- **Lawrence Sutin – *Do What Thou Wilt: A Life of Aleister Crowley***

A balanced and accessible biography that situates Crowley within his cultural and historical context. Sutin emphasizes Crowley's psychological complexity and the evolution of his spiritual philosophy, making it especially useful for readers examining how *Tannhäuser* and *Household Gods* reflect Crowley's shifting views on morality, divinity, and personal will.

- **Gary Lachman – *Aleister Crowley: Magick, Rock and Roll, and the Wickedest Man in the World***

A cultural biography that traces how Crowley's reputation evolved after his death and became a powerful influence on music, counterculture, and modern spirituality. Instead of examining Crowley in his own time, Lachman shows how later generations reframed him, creating a cultural lens through which his earlier writings, including his plays, were reinterpreted and mythologized.

## Occult and Thelemic Commentary

- **Israel Regardie – *The Eye in the Triangle***

Regardie, Crowley's former secretary and student, offers a uniquely intimate portrait of Crowley's inner life—his aspirations, contradictions, and evolving spirituality. Rather than focusing on scandal or mythology, this book illuminates the inward tensions that later surface dramatically in both *Tannhäuser* and *Household Gods*, giving readers a deeper understanding of the spiritual conflicts explored in the plays.

- **Rodney Orpheus** – *Abrahadabra: Understanding Thelema*

A concise and approachable introduction to Thelemic philosophy, written for modern readers. Orpheus clarifies key concepts such as True Will, the Aeons, and ritual structure—making this especially useful for readers of *Tannhäuser* and *Household Gods* who want to understand how Crowley's dramatic works reflect the foundational ideas of Thelema.

- **Rodney Orpheus** – *Thelemic Magick*

Where *Abrahadabra* introduces the philosophy of Thelema, *Thelemic Magick* turns to its practical dimension, explaining how ritual is structured, enacted, and understood in lived spiritual practice. This perspective helps readers recognize how Crowley's use of symbolic action in drama parallels the workings of magick: ideas are not only stated but performed, much as *Tannhäuser* enacts the struggle of will, and *Household Gods* dramatizes spiritual awareness through the everyday.

- **Francis King** – *The Magical World of Aleister Crowley*

A concise and readable overview of Crowley's magical practices, beliefs, and public controversies. King examines the ritual structure underlying Crowley's system, which in turn helps clarify the esoteric architecture framing *Tannhäuser* and *Household Gods,* especially his use of archetype, inversion, and initiatory symbolism.

## Cultural and Religious Analysis

- **Ronald Hutton** – *The Triumph of the Moon: A History of Modern Pagan Witchcraft*

Hutton's landmark study traces the development of modern paganism and the cultural landscape from which Crowley drew. Rather than analyzing Crowley directly, it maps the ritual, mythic, and symbolic currents that later shaped how audiences interpreted his work. For readers of Crowley's plays, it offers a broader view of the esoteric worldview in which his drama was conceived and later received.

- **Nicholas Goodrick-Clarke** – *The Occult Roots of Nazism*

Goodrick-Clarke examines how esoteric and mythological ideas were absorbed into early 20th-century nationalist movements, offering crucial background on the political and symbolic environment in which Crowley was writing. Although Crowley is not the focus, the book shows how occult symbolism was culturally contested and reinterpreted: context that sharpens our understanding of Crowley's satirical and mythic inversions in *Tannhäuser* and *Household Gods*.

- **Marco Pasi** – *Aleister Crowley and the Temptation of Politics*

Pasi offers a rare look at Crowley's political imagination: not as party allegiance, but as a metaphysical question about who (or what) has the right to govern the individual spirit. That insight gives sharper clarity to Crowley's dramatic use of rebellion, moral testing, and spiritual sovereignty, which he dramatizes through characters who must choose between external law and inner will.

## Literary and Dramatic Criticism

- **Tobias Churton** – *Aleister Crowley: The Beast in Berlin*

This biography explores Crowley's years in Weimar-era Berlin: a period of experimental theatre, political volatility, and aggressive artistic reinvention. Churton shows how Berlin's avant-garde culture shaped Crowley's staging instincts, his use of satire, and his belief that ritual performance could be a vehicle for transformation. Understanding this phase of his life gives deeper context to the dramatic sensibility visible in his plays.

- **Tobias Churton** – *Aleister Crowley in America*

This study follows Crowley's time in the United States, where he experimented with new forms of public persona, occult publishing, and spiritual self-presentation. Churton shows how America became a testing ground for Crowley's ideas about performance, authority, and cultural reinvention; these are themes that echo strongly in his dramatic work. His American period reveals how the stage and the self increasingly merged for Crowley, laying the groundwork for the performative dimension of his later writings.

- **Lon Milo DuQuette** – *The Magick of Aleister Crowley: A Handbook of Rituals*

A clear and practical guide to Crowley's ritual work, designed for accessibility without sacrificing precision. DuQuette clarifies the ceremonial logic behind Crowley's symbolism and makes visible the ritual architecture that underlies his dramatic writings; in particular, the way invocation, will, and moral testing are translated into staged action.

## Modern Influence and Reception

- • Hugh Urban – *Magia Sexualis: Sex, Magic, and Liberation in Modern Western Esotericism*

A scholarly examination of the intersection between sexuality and esoteric practice in modern Western traditions. Urban situates Crowley within broader currents of sexual mysticism and countercultural liberation, offering critical context for the erotic and transgressive elements in *Tannhäuser* and *Household Gods*. Particularly useful for readers analyzing how Crowley dramatizes spiritual transformation through sexual symbolism and ritual inversion.

- **Christopher Partridge (ed.) – *The Occult World***

A multidisciplinary collection of essays examining the global impact of occult traditions. Several contributions address Crowley's legacy directly, tracing how his ideas circulated beyond esoteric circles and into literature, art, and cultural experimentation. The volume helps situate Crowley's work within a wider intellectual and religious conversation, showing how the same symbolic and philosophical currents that shape his plays continued to evolve in modern culture.

- **John Symonds – *The Great Beast: The Life and Magick of Aleister Crowley***

An early and sharply critical biography that helped cement Crowley's sensational public image. Hostile in tone but historically influential, it reveals how Crowley's contemporaries misread or exaggerated his theatricality, spirituality, and personal mythmaking. As a document of reception history, it shows how the caricature of "Crowley the monster" formed—and what later readers must look past to understand the meaning and intention behind his dramatic work.

# Film and Media Adaptations

While Aleister Crowley's plays have not been directly adapted for screen, several films and documentaries explore his life, legacy, and esoteric influence. These works vary in tone, fidelity, and interpretive style. Two films titled *Moonchild* are loosely based on Crowley's 1917 novel of the same name, though neither offers a direct adaptation. Readers of the novel will encounter a markedly different experience in tone, structure, and philosophical depth.

## Documentaries and Biographical Films

• *Aleister Crowley: The Wickedest Man in the World* (BBC4, 2002)

A sober and informative documentary narrated by Brian Cox. It traces Crowley's life from religious upbringing to occult experimentation, offering useful context for understanding the philosophical tensions dramatized in *Tannhäuser* and *Household Gods*.

• *The Beast of Loch Ness* (2023)

Focuses on Crowley's time at Boleskine House and its restoration. While not literary, it provides historical background on Crowley's ritual practices and public persona—elements that inform the symbolic structure of his dramatic work.

• *The Confessions of Aleister Crowley* (2020)

A stylized dramatization centered on the Abramelin ritual. Though fictionalized, it reflects Crowley's obsession with spiritual transformation and theatrical self-presentation, themes central to *Tannhäuser*.

## *Moonchild* Adaptations

### • *Moonchild* (1984) – Directed by Genesis P-Orridge

An experimental film referencing Crowley's novel as a symbolic framework. It blends performance art, ritual, and conceptual imagery, originally aired on Spanish television alongside Psychic TV interviews. This version is abstract and esoteric, with no direct narrative correspondence to the novel. Tone and intent differ significantly—where Crowley's *Moonchild* is a satirical magical war with defined characters and philosophical stakes, P-Orridge's film is a visual invocation aimed at transformation.

### • *Moonchild (El Niño de la Luna)* (1989) – Directed by Agustí Villaronga

Loosely inspired by Crowley's novel, this Spanish film reimagines the concept of a magical child within a surreal, cult-driven narrative. It retains thematic elements—spiritual conflict, prophecy, manipulation—but diverges in plot and tone. The film is dreamlike and symbolic, emphasizing mood over doctrinal clarity. Readers of *Moonchild* will find little structural overlap, but may recognize echoes of Crowley's metaphysical concerns.

## Contextual Note on Crowley's Novel

Crowley's *Moonchild* centers on a magical conflict between white and black magicians over the birth of a spiritually charged child. It combines satire, metaphysical speculation, and ritual drama. Neither film adaptation preserves the novel's structure or tone; both reinterpret its core concept through distinct cultural lenses. Readers seeking philosophical coherence, character development, and esoteric framing will find the novel far more direct and instructive than its cinematic counterparts.

# Glossary of Terms

The following glossary defines key terms referenced in *Tannhäuser*, *Household Gods*, and in related essays and commentary on Crowley's occult and philosophical system.

## #

**777** – Crowley's systematic table of magical and Qabalistic correspondences, first published in 1909. *See also* **Qabalah, Tree of Life, Sephiroth.**

## A

**A∴A∴** – The magical order founded by Crowley in 1907, dedicated to the spiritual attainment of the individual through Thelemic initiation. *See also* **Initiation, Thelema, True Will.**

**Abramelin** – A system of ceremonial magic involving invocation of the Holy Guardian Angel, referenced in Crowley's broader magical framework. *See also* **Holy Guardian Angel, Invocation.**

**Adonai** – A Hebrew term for "Lord," used by Crowley symbolically to denote the Higher Self or Holy Guardian Angel.

**Aeon** – A spiritual epoch. Crowley claimed the current Aeon is ruled by Horus, emphasizing individual will and liberation. *See also* **Horus, Thelema.**

**Alchemy** – The spiritual and symbolic art of transformation; Crowley often used alchemical language to describe initiation and union with the divine. *See also* **Transformation, Initiation.**

**Allegory** – A narrative technique in which characters and events symbolically represent abstract ideas; both plays function as allegories for spiritual transformation and philosophical rebellion.

**Astral Plane** – The non-physical realm accessed in ritual and vision; relevant to *The Vision and the Voice* and reflected metaphorically in Crowley's drama. *See also* **Invocation, Egregore.**

# B

**Banishing** – A ritual act to clear or protect space, often used before or after magical work. *See also* **Ritual, Elemental.**

**Baphomet** – A symbolic figure representing duality and occult synthesis; associated with Crowley's reinterpretation of mystical symbols. *See also* **Dualism, Magick.**

**Bethlehem** – Symbolic of dogmatic or sentimental Christianity; sometimes invoked satirically by Crowley to represent spiritual infancy.

# C

**Choronzon** – In Crowley's cosmology, a personification of chaos and ego dissolution encountered during higher ritual work.

**Chorus** – A group voice used in *Tannhäuser* to frame ritual and communal response, echoing classical dramatic structure. *See also* **Metathe-**

atre, Tableau.

# D

**Dualism** – The philosophical tension between body and spirit, sacred and profane—central to both plays. *See also* **Profane vs. Sacred, Eros, Baphomet**.

# E

**Egregore** – A collective thought-form or spiritual entity created by group belief; relevant to symbolic constructs in ritual drama. *See also* **Astral Plane, Invocation**.

**Elemental** – Refers to spirits or forces associated with earth, air, fire, and water; invoked in classical and magical symbolism. *See also* **Banishing, Ritual**.

**Eros** – Symbol of desire, transformation, or divine union; invoked in both plays as a force of disruption and transcendence. *See also* **Dualism, Venus**.

**Eucharist** – In Crowley's system, a symbolic act of spiritual union or transformation, not necessarily Christian in theology; parallels ritual feasts in his plays. *See also* **Ritual, Magick**.

# G

**Gnostic Mass** – A ritual liturgy written by Crowley for the religion of Thelema, echoing Christian structure while subverting its theology. *See also* **Thelema, Ritual Inversion**.

**Grail** – A symbol of spiritual quest and divine union; reinterpreted in *Tannhäuser* as a vessel of personal awakening rather than ecclesiastical salvation. *See also* **Redemption, Eros**.

# H

**Hermeticism** – The esoteric tradition rooted in the teachings attributed to Hermes Trismegistus; forms part of Crowley's intellectual and magical inheritance. *See also* **Alchemy, Magick.**

**Holy Guardian Angel** – In Crowley's system, the higher self or spiritual guide accessed through ritual invocation. *See also* **Abramelin, True Will.**

**Horus** – Egyptian god of war and kingship; central to Crowley's Aeonic theory and symbolic framework. *See also* **Aeon, Osiris.**

**Household Gods** – In the play, refers to domestic deities or symbolic forces that inhabit and disrupt the mundane home environment.

# I

**Idolatry** – The worship of false or symbolic gods; satirized in *Household Gods* as a critique of cultural and religious conformity. *See also* **Satire, Ritual Inversion.**

**Initiation** – A transformative process often dramatized in ritual or symbolic terms; central to Crowley's esoteric system. *See also* **A∴A∴, Alchemy, Transformation.**

**Invocation** – A ritual act of calling upon a deity or spiritual force; used in both plays as a dramatic and metaphysical device. *See also* **Abramelin, Egregore.**

**Isis** – Egyptian goddess of magic and motherhood; often referenced in Crowley's symbolic system. *See also* **Osiris, Horus.**

# K

**Kether / Malkuth** – The highest and lowest sephiroth (emanations) of the Qabalistic Tree of Life, representing divine unity and material manifestation respectively. *See also* **Sephiroth, Tree of Life.**

# L

**Liber** – Title prefix used by Crowley for many of his texts (e.g., *Liber AL vel Legis*); may appear in essays or references.

**Logos** – The divine creative Word; Crowley uses it to denote both the utterance of Will and the principle of spiritual expression through art or ritual.

# M

**Magick** – Crowley's spelling to distinguish spiritual and ritual practice from stage magic; defined as "the Science and Art of causing Change to occur in conformity with Will." *See also* **Thelema, Ritual, True Will.**

**Metatheatre** – Theatre that reflects on itself; relevant to *Household Gods* if interpreted as self-aware ritual performance. *See also* **Stage Directions, Ritual Drama.**

**Mystery Play** – A dramatic form derived from medieval religious drama, used by Crowley as a vehicle for ritual and initiation. *See also* **Ritual Drama, Metatheatre.**

**Mysticism** – Direct experience of the divine; relevant to Crowley's dramatic framing and spiritual philosophy.

# O

**Osiris** – Egyptian god of death and resurrection; symbolic of the previous Aeon superseded by Horus in Crowley's schema. *See also* **Horus, Isis.**

# P

**Pantheon** – A collective of deities; in *Household Gods*, the term refers to the symbolic figures that animate the domestic space.

**Pope Urban IV** – Historical figure referenced in *Tannhäuser*, representing ecclesiastical authority and spiritual judgment.

**Profane vs. Sacred** – A recurring tension in both plays; used to explore inversion, transgression, and spiritual authenticity. *See also* **Dualism, Ritual Inversion**.

# Q

**Qabalah** – The Jewish mystical system adapted by Western occultism; central to Crowley's symbolism. *See also* **Sephiroth, Tree of Life, 777**.

# R

**Redemption** – A theological concept challenged and redefined in *Tannhäuser*, where salvation is not granted by external authority. *See also* **Grail, Profane vs. Sacred**.

**Ritual** – A structured symbolic act intended to produce spiritual or psychological transformation. *See also* **Magick, Banishing, Eucharist, Ritual Drama**.

**Ritual Drama** – A form of theatre in which the performance itself becomes a symbolic or magical operation; central to Crowley's conception of sacred art. *See also* **Metatheatre, Mystery Play**.

**Ritual Inversion** – A technique used by Crowley to subvert traditional religious forms, often by reversing or parodying sacred structures. *See also* **Satire, Profane vs. Sacred**.

# S

**Satire** – A literary mode used in *Household Gods* to critique domesticity, religious dogma, and cultural norms.

**Scarlet Woman** – A Thelemic archetype representing liberated feminine power and active force in ritual and myth. *See also* **Eros, Thelema**.

**Sephiroth** – The ten emanations on the Qabalistic Tree of Life, representing stages of creation and consciousness. *See also* **Kether / Malkuth, Qabalah, Tree of Life**.

**Stage Directions** – In Crowley's plays, often carry symbolic or ritual weight beyond practical staging. *See also* **Metatheatre, Tableau**.

**Star Ruby / Star Sapphire** – Two of Crowley's banishing and invoking rituals; examples of concise ceremonial structure. *See also* **Banishing, Invocation**.

**Symbolic Conflict** – A structural device in which opposing metaphysical or philosophical forces are dramatized through character and action. *See also* **Dualism, Transformation**.

# T

**Tableau** – A staged visual moment; relevant to ritual scenes in *Tannhäuser* and symbolic staging in both plays.

**Tannhäuser** – A medieval German poet and knight; subject of Wagner's opera and Crowley's dramatic inversion. *See also* **Venus, Grail, Redemption**.

**Thelemic Tragedy** – A dramatic form expressing Thelemic principles of self-realization through conflict, initiation, and transcendence. *See also* **Thelema, True Will**.

**Thelema** – Crowley's spiritual philosophy, centered on the principle of discovering and following one's True Will. *See also* **Magick, A∴A∴, True Will**.

**Tree of Life** – The diagrammatic structure of the Qabalah, mapping the relationship between divine and human consciousness. *See also* **Sephiroth, Kether / Malkuth**.

**True Will** – The unique, divinely aligned path of an individual in Thelemic doctrine; a central concept in both plays. *See also* **Thelema, Holy**

**Guardian Angel.**

**Typhonian** – Relating to the darker, chthonic current of Egyptian symbolism within Crowley's cosmology; occasionally reflected in his dramatic imagery. *See also* **Horus, Osiris.**

# V

**Venus** – Roman goddess of love and desire; in *Tannhäuser*, she represents both temptation and metaphysical initiation. *See also* **Eros, Venusberg.**

**Venusberg** – A mythic realm of sensual pleasure; reimagined in *Tannhäuser* as a site of spiritual confrontation. *See also* **Venus, Redemption.**

.

www.ingramcontent.com/pod-product-compliance
Lightning Source LLC
La Vergne TN
LVHW041247080426
835510LV00009B/629